THE INVENTION OF THE BIBLICAL SCHOLAR

"*A* lively and readable survey of the engagement of literary and biblical studies with Theory, that is, postmodern theories. The authors challenge biblical scholars to engage Theory to understand our own disciplinary history, and thereby widen our horizons and free ourselves to be more broadly intellectually relevant. I encourage biblical scholars and graduate students to take up the challenge."

—Joanna Dewey
Harvey H. Guthrie Jr. Professor Emerita of Biblical Studies
Episcopal Divinity School, Cambridge, Massachusetts

THE
INVENTION
OF THE
BIBLICAL
SCHOLAR

A
CRITICAL
MANIFESTO

Stephen D. Moore
and
Yvonne Sherwood

Fortress Press
MINNEAPOLIS

THE INVENTION OF THE BIBLICAL SCHOLAR
A Critical Manifesto

Cover image: © Radius Images/Corbis
Cover design: Brad Norr Design
Book design: Ann Delgehausen, Trio Bookworks

Library of Congress Cataloging-in-Publication Data
Moore, Stephen D.
   The invention of the biblical scholar : a critical manifesto / Stephen Moore and Yvonne Sherwood.
      p. cm.
   ISBN 978-0-8006-9774-7 (alk. paper)
   1. Bible—Criticism, interpretation, etc.—History.   2. Critical theory—History.   I. Sherwood, Yvonne.   II. Title.
   BS500.M655 2011
   220.072—dc22

                                                          2010044875
The paper used in this publication meets the minimum requirements of American National Standard for Information Sciences—Permanence of Paper for Printed Library Materials, ANSI Z329.48-1984.

Manufactured in the U.S.A.

Contents

Acknowledgments

The authors would like to thank Ken Stone and the steering committee of the Reading, Theory and the Bible Section of the SBL for the initial provocation of the "After Theory" panel, and Fiona Black and the steering committee of the Biblical Criticism and Literary Criticism Section for providing us with a forum to present a second installment of our ideas. Thanks are also due to Thomas Fabisiak for sharing his pre-published work on eighteenth-century biblical scholarship with us, and to Ward Blanton who, at the Glasgow end, made a crucial contribution to the development of certain ideas. Above all, we are thankful to Neil Elliott at Fortress Press for his enthusiasm and support for this project, even in its still inchoate stages, and to the entire Fortress Press production team for seeing it speedily into print.

Trial-balloon versions of much of the material in this book have appeared in *Biblical Interpretation* as follows: "Biblical Studies 'after' Theory: Onwards Towards the Past; Part One: After 'after Theory,' and Other Apocalyptic Conceits," *Biblical Interpretation* 18:1 (2010): 1–27; "Part Two: The Secret Vices of the Biblical God," *Biblical Interpretation* 18:2 (2010): 87–113; "Part Three: Theory in the First and Second Waves," *Biblical Interpretation* 18:3 (2010): 191–225. The authors are grateful to E. J. Brill, publisher of the journal, for permission to reprint the material in revised and expanded form.

Preface

THE IRREDUCIBLE STRANGENESS OF THE BIBLICAL SCHOLAR

This immodest manifesto began life as a modest conference paper. Entitled "After 'After Theory,' and Other Apocalyptic Conceits in Literary and Biblical Studies," it was part of a joint AAR/SBL session[1] convened to consider the consequences for biblical studies of the alleged—indeed, widely trumpeted—demise of poststructuralist theory ("Theory" for short) in literary studies. As two biblical scholars long associated with Theory, we might have been expected (might even have expected ourselves) to utter a fairly perfunctory lament that Theory was still widely perceived as a rather distant satellite orbiting the historical-critical core of the biblical studies discipline, and now that satellite seemed in danger of disintegrating without ever having come close enough to register on the hermeneutical horizons of most biblical scholars. Somewhat to our relief, however, a more interesting project than lament emerged in the course of writing the paper. Precisely by thinking the history and practices of our discipline from a tangent—and what could be more tangential to the waking interests of the average biblical scholar than poststructuralist theory?—we began to reimagine the genealogy and machinery of our discipline in ways that were unfamiliar, not least to

---

1. Specifically (and more long-windedly), it was a joint session of the Bible, Theology, and Postmodernity Group and the Reading, Theory, and the Bible Section held at the Joint Annual Meeting of the American Academy of Religion and the Society of Biblical Literature at San Diego, California, in November 2007.

ourselves. In the counterintuitive history of biblical scholarship that results, historical criticism and literary criticism do not take up their habitual roles as perpetual sparring partners, even when the literary criticism in question is armed with poststructuralist theory. Instead, historical criticism and literary criticism are both seen as contributing to the distinctly modern phenomenon that historian Jonathan Sheehan has termed "the Enlightenment Bible."

The irreducible strangeness of the biblical scholar is the central topic of this brief book. The book tells the tale of the invention of a particular and peculiar academic entity—the professional biblical scholar—and provides a defamiliarizing redescription of what he or she is uniquely designed to do. The book is not a traditional history of historical-critical biblical scholarship as an aetiological saga in which the authentically "historical" and "critical" identity markers arrive in increments until the features in the emerging portrait have transformed into our own. Nor is it a saga of latter-day redemption in which the (literary-)Theoretical arrives, however belatedly, to save us from a sclerotic history-obsessed legacy, though we ourselves, admittedly, have delighted in spinning such soteriological stories in the past. On this occasion, we prefer to sidestep these oft-recited narratives to ask certain fundamental but under-examined questions. Why, in early modernity, did the scholarly mind come to associate the Bible so determinedly with history? Why did the "criticism" in biblical criticism resolutely and exclusively come to take the form of *historical* criticism? What other forms might biblical criticism have taken? What forgotten forms did early modern biblical criticism actually take? What untried forms might biblical criticism yet take?

Responding to a loss of theological authority, the Bible was rehabilitated on human and cultural grounds in the eighteenth century. The Bible was re-universalized, so to speak, and its relevance newly perpetuated in such unlikely domains as philology, ancient history, archaeology, ancient Near Eastern languages, and the quest for the ever-elusive authorial hand. The zones of potential inquiry were myriad but also severely circumscribed, not least because the emerging discipline eventually set aside and repressed what we are calling "moral critique"—critique of the morality of certain biblical material and even of the biblical God—though such critique had featured prominently in the discipline's earlier stages, as we show. This repressed terrain does not ordinarily appear in standard histories of the discipline, even though its relationship to contemporary politicized forms of biblical scholarship, such as feminist, ideological, and postcolonial forms, is profound.

But the phenomenon of the Enlightenment Bible has profound ramifications for other aspects of contemporary biblical scholarship as well. We argue that the entire series of biblical-scholarly raids on (mainly literary) Theory has been conducted in the long shadow of the Enlightenment Bible. What we term the "first wave" of Theory in biblical studies extended the project of the Enlightenment Bible and invested it with new energy. Biblical literary criticism was largely dedicated to the retrieval of the Bible as a supreme work of human artistry, while biblical cultural studies demonstrated, even celebrated, the Bible's cultural ubiquity and hence its abiding cultural relevance. But the reach of the Enlightenment Bible extended even farther. In the first wave of its reception in biblical studies, Theory was treated as "secular" demystifying stuff that enabled even ostensibly postmodern biblical scholars to carry on the early modern task of translating the "religious" into human terms and cultural categories.

Ironically, these developments overlapped with an unlikely turn in Theory that began in earnest in the 1990s—the deployment of religion and the Bible by thinkers not themselves religionists or biblical scholars to unsettle the givenness of the "human" and the "secular." This Theoretical "turn to religion" has since been supplemented by historical and analytic inquiry into the formation of fundamental modern categories such as secularism and critique. And it seems to us that it is here, at this very curious and specific interdisciplinary intersection, that biblical studies has most to contribute, and most to gain, in its engagement with Theory. What biblical studies most stands to gain, and needs to gain, we would argue, is a certain turn—a certain return—to philosophy. If Theorists have been staging a turn to religion, and even theology, to unsettle and spook philosophy, then Theory-inclined biblical scholars ought to stage a return to philosophy via Theory to unsettle and spook the disciplinary status quo, philosophy being another repressed element that figured prominently in the formative phase of the discipline, as we also show.

The return of philosophy to biblical studies, however, has already occurred in part. An important reason why Theory has proved so attractive to some biblical scholars is that it has offered a means of reconnecting to certain basic questions of philosophy that had been part and parcel of educated public response to the Bible in the eighteenth and even nineteenth centuries, but that became severed from biblical studies when the discipline began to fixate more narrowly on the historical (for reasons we attempt to explain), understood increasingly in a fervently exclusivist sense. The early manifestations of a return of philosophy to biblical studies via Theory, however, were often naïve. The revelation that knowledge of the object (in this case, the biblical text) can only ever be mediated by the subject, and hence objectivity by subjectivity, was trumpeted as a postmodern epiphany in work that was frequently oblivious to how such issues had been hotly-debated ones for philosophy when biblical scholarship was still in its infancy.

But the fact that an attack on the phantom of "objectivity" was seen as one of the most unsettling challenges for biblical scholarship showed to what extent the latter had become the ultimate discipline for enacting scrupulous separation between the observing subject and the religious object—together with all the machinery of "objectivity," "neutrality," and "disinterestedness" that went along with it (even if many historical critics now try to throw a cover over the machinery). What other discipline in the humanities has striven more determinedly to perform the separation of the properly critical subject from the properly studied object? What other discipline has been more anxious to separate the professional from the confessional, the public from the personal, through the development of ever more meticulously honed critical tools? What other discipline has been more fixated on "method" in consequence? Loud battles between "believing" and "unbelieving" biblical scholars may well be as far from the substance of the matter as battles between the historical critics and the literary critics. For almost all biblical scholarship has been enacted within the massive edifice of the Enlightenment Bible, it seems to us, by which we mean that almost all biblical scholars have thoroughly internalized Enlightenment modes of relating to the Bible—modes anxiously marked as distinct from the devotional and the confessional, the pietistic and the homiletical, through a fetishistic display of methodological expertise as the primary badge of professional identity.

Paradoxically, however, it is precisely this oddly fraught location that now positions biblical scholarship to make its most important contribution to contemporary academic debate. One of the principal challenges of Theory in the "second wave" will be to denaturalize and defamiliarize the discipline of biblical studies, to engender metacritical reflection that asks why the professional study of the Bible took the particular and peculiar forms that it has and how it might be different than it is. Such defamiliarizing histories of the discipline will need to traverse more complex terrain than flashbulb moments of genius occurring now and then in the minds of individual biblical scholars in Germany, Britain, or France. Biblical scholarship, then or now, cannot be thought independently of social, cultural, and political space—the very separation of the "social," "political," and "cultural" from the "religious" being an effect produced by, among other things, nascent biblical scholarship, hence its relevance to wider academic debate. Rethinking the history of biblical scholarship in such ways will help us understand how moderns have constructed the social, the cultural, the political, and the religious—and potentially help us to reconfigure those intractable configurations. A discipline that is constantly distinguishing itself from the pre-critical and pre-modern (and now from the postmodern as well) and relating its own genesis to the epiphany of the modern and critical in early modern Europe clearly has much to contribute to contemporary discussion about the formulation and reification of some of the primary categories and dichotomies of modernity. These include the public and the private, the secular and the religious, the rational and the supernatural, the universal and the particular, the historical and the theological, the philosophical and the theological, the critical and the pre-critical, and the human and its others, both animal and divine.

As Theory is to biblical studies, so biblical studies is to modernity (especially as epitomized by the academy). Both appear peripheral and tangential, and either too minor to merit an apocalypse or even a funeral or so well into their dotage that one can simply sit back and await their inevitable demise. In both cases, however, it proves extremely productive to think the dominant phenomenon—biblical studies on the one hand, modernity on the other—in relation to that which it imagines most minor, moribund, irrelevant, a matter of private interest only. We can learn most about biblical studies and modernity by looking at what they most want to die or consider essentially dead.

We asked the candidate what her dream course would be, and she said she would like to teach a course in "theory and—and, um—" (there was a long silence) "theory and *non*theory." Our chair asked, "*non*theory, what's that?" And she said, "well, nontheory—like, *you* know, poems, stories, plays." And he said, "Oh yes, what we used to call literature."[1]

Literary "theory" was pronounced dead today by the Association of Literary Scholars and Critics' Ad Hoc Committee on the Status of Interpretation.[2]

Theory itself is only too happy to witness the passing of Theory. Nothing stimulates the production of Theory like the proclamation of its own death.[3]

THEORY
AND
METHODOLATRY

Theory's Obituaries

By the mid-1980s, poststructuralism had become the dominant discourse in U.S. literary studies[4]—a rather sad and curious fate for a congeries of critical positions that, collectively, made so much of the marginal and the peripheral and relentlessly subjected dominant discourses to principled interrogation.[5] Eugene Goodheart, long a critic of poststructuralism, nuances its ascent in the 1970s and 1980s:

> What I am describing did not occur everywhere in the academy. I suspect that many institutions of higher learning in the country have not experienced an academic transformation, and that there are still places where the older traditions of teaching prevail. . . . But the transformation did take place in the leading institutions which have a disproportionate influence not only on the academic, but also on the cultural life generally.[6]

---

1. Sandra Gilbert, "New Uses for Old Boys: An Interview with Sandra Gilbert," in *Professions: Conversations on the Future of Literary and Cultural Studies*, ed. Donald E. Hall (Urbana and Chicago: University of Illinois Press, 2001), 252.

2. Michael Bérubé, "Literary Theory Is Dead and I Feel Fine," January 28, 2004: http://www.michaelberube.com/index.php/weblog/literary_theory_is_dead_and_i_feel_fine/ (accessed May 14, 2010).

3. Martin McQuillan, Graeme MacDonald, Robin Purves, and Stephen Thomson, "The Joy of Theory," in *Post-Theory: New Directions in Criticism*, ed. Martin McQuillan et al. (Edinburgh: Edinburgh University Press, 1999), ix.

4. "Literary studies" is a term of convenience. "Departments of literary studies" are few or non-existent, at any rate in the Anglophone world. The term "literary studies," as ordinarily used, denotes the bread-and-butter activity of modern language departments (English, French, Spanish, etc.) and departments of comparative literature.

5. Deconstruction was the most visible variant of poststructuralism, and entailed the dismantling of "metaphysical" concepts (origin, essence, identity, etc.) and hierarchical oppositions (presence/absence, central/marginal, masculine/feminine, etc.); exposure of the exclusions, omissions, and blind spots that enable texts, and entire societies, to function; and analysis of the ways in which literary, critical, and philosophical arguments are destabilized by the figural language (metaphor, metonymy, synecdoche, etc.) on which they rely. The next most prominent variant of poststructuralism in the mid-1980s was the Foucauldian; in the succeeding decade, however, it would come to overshadow the deconstuctive variants. It specialized in unearthing the constructedness of some of the most-solid seeming features of the Western cultural landscape, not least sexuality. Accessible introductions to poststructuralism include Catherine Belsey, *Poststructuralism: A Very Short Introduction* (Oxford: Oxford University Press, 2002), and James Williams, *Understanding Poststructuralism* (Chesham, U.K.: Acumen, 2005).

6. Eugene Goodheart, *Does Literary Studies Have a Future?* (Madison, Wis.: University of Wisconsin Press, 1999), 20–21.

The institutionalization of poststructuralism within the Modern Language Association[7] received vivid symbolic expression in 1986 with the election of arch-deconstructionist J. Hillis Miller to its presidency. For quite some time, in short, poststructuralism has occupied a role in U.S. literary studies not unlike that of historical criticism in biblical studies as the *sine qua non* for initiation into the discipline.

Poststructuralism has also long epitomized "high theory" in literary studies—or "Theory" as we shall term it for convenience. Poststructuralism's relationship to Theory has generally been synecdochic, the part standing in for the whole.[8] It is no accident that Theory's most visible early outing as a term was in Jonathan Culler's *On Deconstruction*, a book that arguably did more than any other to popularize deconstruction, a frequent synecdoche in turn for poststructuralism, in Anglo-American literary studies. As the book opens we find Culler ruminating on how "works of literary theory are [now] closely and vitally related to other writings within a domain as yet unnamed but often called 'theory' for short. This domain is not 'literary theory,'" continues Culler, "since many of its most interesting works do not explicitly address literature. . . . [T]he most convenient designation is simply the name 'theory.'"[9] More recently, Culler has defined Theory as an umbrella term for "discourses that come to exercise influence outside their apparent disciplinary realm because they offer new and persuasive characterizations of problems or phenomena of general interest: language, consciousness, meaning, nature and culture, the functioning of the psyche, the relations of individual experience to larger structures, and so on."[10]

Since the 1980s, the term "Theory," at once vague and specific, has stood in for a paradoxically expansive yet selective body of work: Russian formalism, French structuralism, semiotics, poststructuralism, deconstruction, Lacanian and post-Lacanian psychoanalytic theory,

---

7. The principal professional association within the field(s) of literary studies, its annual convention regularly attracting more than ten thousand attendees.

8. In hindsight it is being asked why Theory was "collapsed into the synecdoche of poststructuralism" and whether it even makes sense to postulate poststructuralism as a "unitary phenomenon." See Judith Butler, John Guillory, and Kendall Thomas, "Preface," in *What's Left of Theory? New Work on the Politics of Literary Theory*, ed. Judith Butler et al. (London and New York: Routledge, 2000), viii.

9. Jonathan Culler, *On Deconstruction: Theory and Criticism after Structuralism* (Ithaca, N.Y.: Cornell University Press, 1982), 8.

10. Jonathan Culler, *The Literary in Theory* (Cultural Memory in the Present; Stanford, Calif.: Stanford University Press, 2007), 4.

assorted Marxisms and neo-Marxisms, reader-response criticism and *Rezeptionsästhetik*, "French feminist theory" (more precisely, *écriture féminine*), "third-wave" feminist theory, gender studies, queer theory, New Historicism, cultural materialism, cultural studies, postcolonial studies, and (academic) postmodernism *tout court*, along with carefully selected slices of what is known (often polemically) as "continental philosophy." Theory's national origins are thus seen to lie quite specifically in a transatlantic alliance between France and the United States with walk-on parts for a few Russians, Germans, and Italians, and a brief detour through Birmingham (England, not Alabama) for cultural studies. Theory's A-list has included such assorted luminaries as Jacques Derrida, Michel Foucault, Jacques Lacan, Roland Barthes, Julia Kristeva, Louis Althusser, Gilles Deleuze, Luce Irigaray, Paul de Man, Edward Said, Fredric Jameson, Gayatri Chakravorty Spivak, Judith Butler, Homi Bhabha, Slavoj Žižek, and Donna Haraway, to name but a few representative figures. Theory does not include figures like Jung or Weber; it may not even include figures like Adorno or Habermas.[11] And though its corpus is corpulent and expansive, Theory is hardly a single body. In its relatively short life it has seen as many sectarian schisms as post-Reformation Christianity. Proponents of cultural materialism, say, are as prone to parody New Historicists, or neo-Marxists to parody postcolonial theorists, as evangelical Christians are to parody Roman Catholics—or other evangelical Christians. Not surprisingly, therefore, attacks on Theory have been equally conflicted, with Theory serving as a repository for mutually exclusive accusations. Charged with being at once too high (arcane, scholastic, esoteric) and too low (vulgar, materialist, pop-cultural), Theory has become a target for both "right" and "left," at once too "politically correct" and too apolitical, remote, and disengaged.

Thus far we have been writing as though Theory still ruled the roost in literary studies, but its hold has slackened, seemingly, in recent years. "High theory," epitomized by poststructuralist theory, is currently in a state of perceived decline. In the field of literary studies, book titles such as *Post-Theory, After Theory, Reading after Theory*, and *What's Left*

---

11. For the filleted version of Theory and what it excludes, see Amanda Anderson, *The Way We Argue Now: A Study in the Cultures of Theory* (Princeton, N.J.: Princeton University Press, 2006), 1.

of Theory?[12] suggest that Theory is currently croaking its last gasp—though closer inspection suggests that certain of those trumpeting Theory's demise most loudly may also be standing over Theory with a pillow, intent on bringing about the very death they are describing. Even for the authors of these would-be obituaries, however,[13] what has taken or will take Theory's place is still veiled from view, awaiting apocalypse. Introducing *After Theory*, eponymous exemplar of the "after Theory" phenomenon and arguably its most influential product, Terry Eagleton cautions:

> Those to whom the title of this book suggests that "theory" is now over, and that we can all relievedly return to an age of pre-theoretical innocence, are in for a disappointment. There can be no going back to an age when it was enough to pronounce Keats delectable or Milton a doughty spirit. It is not as though the whole project was a ghastly mistake on which some merciful soul has now blown the whistle, so that we can all return to whatever it was we were doing before Ferdinand de Saussure heaved over the horizon.[14]

12. McQuillan et al., *Post-Theory*; Thomas Docherty, *After Theory* (Edinburgh: Edinburgh University Press, 1996); Terry Eagleton, *After Theory* (New York: Basic, 2003); Valentine Cunningham, *Reading after Theory* (Blackwell Manifestos; Oxford: Wiley-Blackwell, 2002); Butler, Guillory, and Thomas, *What's Left of Theory?* See also Jacques Derrida, Frank Kermode, Toril Moi, and Christopher Norris, *Life.after.theory* (New York: Continuum, 2004), a book whose engagement with the "after Theory" debate is more oblique. For the proceedings of a particularly public would-be postmortem on Theory conducted in Chicago in April 2003 by a particularly distinguished group of Theorists, see "The Future of Criticism: A Critical Inquiry Symposium," *Critical Inquiry* 30 (2004): 324–483. As the editors of *Post-Theory* astutely remark, the death of Theory seems to have become "a persistent theme *in* Theory" (McQuillan et al., "The Joy of Theory," ix, their emphasis). With the announced demise of Theory in general, moreover, questions are now being asked as to whether specific types of Theory, some until recently deemed hale and hearty, are also at death's door; see, for example, "The End of Postcolonial Theory? A Roundtable with Sunil Agnani, Fernando Coronil, Gaurav Desai, Mamadou Diouf, Simon Gikandi, Susie Tharu, and Jennifer Wenzel," *PMLA* 122 (2007): 633–51.

13. Speaking of obituaries, see in addition Paul Bové, *In the Wake of Theory* (Middletown, Conn.: Wesleyan University Press, 1992), and Barbara Johnson, *The Wake of Deconstruction* (The Bucknell Lectures in Literary Theory, 11; Oxford: Blackwell, 1994).

14. Eagleton, *After Theory*, 1–2. Further still on Theory's rise and alleged decline, see Dwight Eddins, ed., *The Emperor Redressed: Critiquing Critical Theory* (Tuscaloosa: University of Alabama Press, 1995); Wendell V. Harris, *Beyond Poststructuralism: The*

The very debate engendered by Eagleton and others, however, serves to create a sense of Theory as, at the very least, an "obtrusive ghost" in literary studies.[15]

Or is it literature instead that is the ghost in literary studies? "A specter is haunting the academy, the specter of literature," Marjorie Perloff announced in her 2006 MLA presidential address.[16] She was lamenting the dramatic demise of literary knowledge among students of literature. "I have heard graduate students discussing the vagaries of Romantic self-consciousness in Shelley's 'Ode to the West Wind,'" she complains, "who cannot tell you what an ode is, what apostrophe is, or why (much less how) this one is written in terza rima."[17] She continues: "But whose fault is this? Not that of theory, for consider . . . the excellent theorists, from Roman Jakobson and William Empson to Hélène Cixous and Julia Kristeva, who have written superb critical commentary on particular poems."[18] The problem with these unlettered students of literature, it would seem, is that they swallow the Theory but spit out the criticism, and with it the literariness of the literary work. Precisely two decades, then, after J. Hillis Miller's deconstructive MLA presidential address, which, as we noted earlier, marked the official arrival of Theory, flushed with triumph, in the literary studies academy,[19] Perloff's MLA

Speculations of Theory and the Experience of Reading (University Park: Pennsylvania State University Press, 1996); and especially Daphne Patai and Will H. Corral, eds., *Theory's Empire: An Anthology of Dissent* (New York: Columbia University Press, 2005), about which we have much to say below.

15. Jean-Michel Rabaté, *The Future of Theory* (Oxford: Blackwell, 2002), 10.

16. Marjorie Perloff, "Presidential Address 2006: It Must Change," *PMLA* 122 (2007): 658.

17. Ibid. Biblical-scholarly versions of this lament would not be hard to imagine: "I have heard graduate students discussing the vagaries of rhetorical purpose in Paul's Letter to the Galatians who cannot tell you what forensic rhetoric is, how it differs from epideictic or deliberative rhetoric, or why (much less how) Paul adapts all or any of these oratorical techniques in his letter. . . ."

18. Ibid. Here Perloff is echoing Terry Eagleton's *How to Read a Poem* (Oxford: Blackwell, 2007), 2. She begins this section of her address by quoting one of Eagleton's opening quips: "I first thought of writing this book when I realized that hardly any of the students of literature I encountered these days practiced what I myself had been trained to regard as literary criticism. Like thatching or clog dancing, literary criticism seems to be something of a dying art" (ibid, 1).

19. Delivered in 1986, the address was published the following year as J. Hillis Miller, "The Triumph of Theory, the Resistance to Reading, and the Question of the Material Base," *PMLA* 102 (1987): 281–91.

presidential address is attempting, politely but firmly, to help Theory into its coat and usher it out the door as a guest that has overstayed its welcome.[20] Indeed, Perloff, like Eagleton, is convinced that Theory is, in any case, already on its way out. She notes how not so long ago,

> "everyone" had to know Marx and Freud, Benjamin and Adorno, Foucault and Derrida, Lacan and Kristeva. But increasingly this Eurocentric theory has come to seem less than adequate for dealing with the growing body of minority, transnational, and postcolonial literature, and so poststructuralist theory is being replaced by critical race studies and related models, but so eclectic have the categories become that in most colleges and universities there is now no theory requirement at all.[21]

Perloff may, however, be indulging in wishful thinking here; for prominent among these "related models" are sundry politicized forms of poststructuralism, however eclectic and generic that poststructuralism may have become in the process of its dissemination and politicization. The problem for Theory-weary discontents like Perloff is that Theory has seeped so deeply into the soil of literary studies that it is now all but impossible to dig around or under it. Michael Bérubé argues the case with regard to deconstruction, once Theory's most alluring product, now hopelessly outdated, even dead, yet still eerily alive:

> [Y]ou don't really need to know this or that text by Derrida in order to make your way through graduate school or the profession at large. However, and this is a seriously italic "however," you should be aware that deconstruction has seeped into the groundwater of the discipline, even as the term itself lost any distinct referent long ago. It has been "disseminated," in fact, in just the way that deconstruction itself suggests: the word is now floating around

---

20. Theory's first conspicuous sighting in America is commonly dated to 1966 (see p. 16 below), two decades before Miller's presidential address. The tale of Theory in America, then, is one whose plot unfolds in twenty-year cycles so regular as to cause the pulse of a premillenial dispensationalist to race.

21. Perloff, "Presidential Address 2006," 656.

out there, and cannot be recalled to its point of origin. . . . You don't need to be able to cite Derrida's *Dissemination* chapter and verse. But you do need to know what a deconstructive argument looks and sounds like, and you need to know what implicit and explicit claims are at stake in such an argument, because you will encounter these arguments in essays and books where they will not declare their names. . . . [O]ver the past thirty years, these arguments have been as common as rain, and they've seeped into the disciplinary groundwater.[22]

Even if deconstruction and other forms of Theory can in some sense be said to be "dead," then, in no sense can they be said to be gone.

Reports of Theory's recent or imminent demise, in any case, even assuming they are not exaggerated,[23] are not good news, it seems to us, for biblical critics with pronounced interests in literary studies. For Theory has long functioned as a kind of lingua franca in our particular sector of the humanities. The absorption of "Theory" back into "reading" and the corresponding decentering of Theory and Theoreticians in favour of a renewed foregrounding of literature and literary authors may be cheering news indeed for Theory-weary literary critics, but hardly for biblical literary critics restlessly searching for ever-new angles on the same old set of texts. For the lightning bolt of inspiration is, on the whole, far more likely to strike the biblical critic browsing works with such titles as *Deconstructions: A User's Guide*, or *Queer Studies: An Interdisciplinary Reader*, or *Postcolonialisms: An Anthology of Cultural Theory and Criticism* than browsing works with such titles as *The Art of Shakespeare's Sonnets*, or *Jane Austen's Letters*, or *T. S. Eliot: His Mind and Personality*.[24]

---

22. Michael Bérubé, "Conventional Wisdom," *Profession* (2009): 17–18, n. 1.

23. Colin Davis, for one, in *After Poststructuralism: Reading, Stories and Theory* (London and New York: Routledge, 2004), argues that such reports *are* exaggerated and that Theory will continue to play a crucial role in the humanities. So too Peter Barry, whose *Continuing Theory* (3rd ed.; Manchester: Manchester University Press, 2009) also engages the "after Theory" debate. As the book's title suggests, Barry is himself not ready to pull the plug on Theory. Neither are the contributors to Derek Attridge and Jane Elliott, eds., *Theory after "Theory"* (London and New York: Routledge, 2010), a recent major collection that projects a rich (after)life for Theory beyond the older poststructuralisms.

24. Nicholas Royle, ed., *Deconstructions: A User's Guide* (New York: Palgrave Macmillan, 2000); Robert J. Corber and Stephen Valocchi, eds., *Queer Studies: An Inter-*

In biblical studies, in any case, Theory hardly faces the same mortal threat as in literary studies. Theory can hardly be said to have risen to sufficiently Luciferian heights in biblical studies to undergo any meaningful fall. Rather than being cast from the celestial heights, it would have to be thrown from a basement window. Theory-weary book titles are hardly a fixture of contemporary biblical studies. We do not find biblical scholars reflexively reaching for the particular eschatological trope of Theory's Decline and Fall to limn an as yet dimly glimpsed future designed, as all such futures are, to reorient the present polemically. The first reason for this is the obvious one: any call for an apocalypse of Theory from within biblical studies would sound absurd. Apocalypses are not minor fires started by pyromaniacs, but last-ditch emergency measures, reserved for overbearing worlds that need imagining otherwise. To get a decent apocalyptic fire going you need something momentous and massive (the Roman Empire, say, would do nicely; the American Empire would do just as well) to send up in flames.

Academics are as adept as any other constituency at imagining themselves as members of a beleaguered minority. Books or articles written from an acknowledged perspective of privilege and majority are ever in short supply. That being said, visions of victimhood can only go so far. The image of traditionally minded biblical scholars marooned in a small rowing boat or huddling on a small island on a globe that has been thoroughly colonized by Theory would sound paranoid and absurd. "Theory's Empire" in biblical studies is approximately the size of Tobago or the Falkland Islands. This is the underwhelming reality that John J. Collins is up against in his *The Bible after Babel*, a rare biblical studies contribution to the "After Theory" subgenre. But even Collins is compelled to admit a few pages into his book: "It is not the case that the postmodernists have captured the field. Far from it."[25]

---

disciplinary Reader (Oxford: Wiley-Blackwell, 2003); Gaurav Desai and Supriya Nair, eds., *Postcolonialisms: An Anthology of Cultural Theory* (New Brunswick, N.J.: Rutgers University Press, 2005); Helen Vendler, *The Art of Shakespeare's Sonnets* (Cambridge, Mass.: Belknap Press, 1999); Jane Austen, *Jane Austen's Letters*, ed. Deirdre Le Faye (Oxford: Oxford University Press, 1995); S. S. Hoskot, *T. S. Eliot: His Mind and Personality* (Philadelphia: Richard West, 1979).

25. John J. Collins, *The Bible after Babel: Historical Criticism in a Postmodern Age* (Grand Rapids, Mich.: Eerdmans, 2005), 3. Similar in tone is James Barr, *History and Ideology in the Old Testament: Biblical Studies at the End of a Millenium* (2nd ed.; Oxford: Oxford University Press, 2005). The faint apocalypticism of the book's subtitle

Far from it, indeed, especially when the field is set in international perspective. Biblical scholars from the global South have tended to have an uneasy relationship with academic postmodernism, epitomized by Theory. European biblical scholars have tended to have a more straightforward relationship with it: most of them have dismissed it outright. The leading European professional associations for biblical studies offer far fewer forums for the non-traditionalist than the (American-based) Society of Biblical Literature. The Studiorum Novi Testamenti Societas, for instance, has never even had a program unit devoted to garden-variety feminist biblical hermeneutics, much less its third-wave, Theory-infused mutations.[26] European biblical scholarship in general groans under the burden of a long and glorious history. Bent over so far is it under the weight of this history that it habitually looks backward between its bowed legs. Even in the United States, however, biblical scholars with serious interests in literary theory, critical theory, cultural theory, or other related domains tend to be isolated voices—when not absent altogether—from the principal Ph.D.-granting institutions, graduate programs at such institutions still being shaped primarily by traditional historical-critical agendas.[27] The situation of Theory in biblical studies is thus diametrically opposed to its situation in literary studies. In the latter field, as noted above, Theory early took up its abode in the most prestigious U.S. departments and programs, and trickled out from there to saturate the field, the stream gradually swelling into a flood.

And yet there has been progress of a sort in biblical studies. Few if any of the first generation of biblical literary critics emerged from their respective doctoral programs with any real degree of fluency in the second language of Theory. For certain of them, indeed, the discovery of Theory—for the most part, literary theory—was a Damascus

---

is amplified in certain of its chapters, particularly the one entitled "Postmodernism" (141–62).

26. What SNTS has had most years, since around 1980, is one "... And Everything Else" program unit (or "seminar," as the units are called)—but only one at a time, to balance the fifteen or so other seminars devoted to traditional historical criticism, untainted by any touch of Theory. This "... And Everything Else" seminar has assumed various titles. Two of the longer-lived have been "The Role of the Reader in the Interpretation of the New Testament" (1985–1993) and "Hermeneutics and the Biblical Text" (1994–1999). At the time of writing, its title is "New Challenges for New Testament Hermeneutics in the 21st Century."

27. Cf. Dale Martin, *Pedagogy of the Bible: An Analysis and Proposal* (Louisville, Ky.: Westminster John Knox, 2008), 15.

road encounter experienced after they had exited graduate school alto-gether and begun to publish as historical critics. In more recent years, in marked contrast, a significant number of graduate students seem already to be fluently bilingual, shuttling between the discourses of bib-lical and literary studies with an ease not always shared by their doc-toral mentors. Related to this development, no doubt, is the fact that the time-warp factor, long so pronounced in biblical literary criticism, has noticeably decreased. By this we mean that deconstruction and other forms of poststructuralism, such as New Historicism, were not taken up in biblical studies until long after their first flowering, and even their eventual decline, in literary studies, whereas most of the major devel-opments of the 1990s in literary studies, in contrast—cultural studies, postcolonial studies, queer theory, masculinity studies, autobiographi-cal criticism—had all been taken up in biblical studies even before that decade had come to an end.[28] Contemporary biblical literary critics tend, on the whole, to be more attuned to real-time literary studies than their time-traveling predecessors.

Theory in the Cafeteria

Through our (admittedly jaundiced) eyes, however, Theory, while certainly alive and sometimes even kicking in biblical studies, seems all too often to be used as garnish, a soupçon of Zeitgeist spice, on modes of critical practice that remain fundamentally unaffected by it; or it tends to circulate among a few overworked usual suspects and fervent new recruits who preach to the converted in the Theory-ghettos of the Society of Biblical Literature annual meeting. Definitely not a Tower of Babel, then; with so few builders it has long since set its sights considerably lower than the heavens.

But even this modest building project has recently been curtailed. In 2002, the Research and Publications Committee of the SBL shut down *Semeia: An Experimental Journal for Biblical Criticism* against the pro-tests of its editorial board. *Semeia* and the *Journal of Biblical Literature* had, for some years previously, constituted the society's two official jour-nals.[29] (The reverse scenario, a pulling of the plug on *JBL* leaving *Semeia*

---

28. We discuss these appropriations below.

29. At the time of writing, two other journals have replaced *Semeia* on the journals page of the SBL website (https://www.sbl-site.org/publications/browsejournals.aspx).

to represent the entire society, would, of course, be unimaginable.) *Semeia*'s founding in 1974 under the auspices of the SBL represented Theory's first conspicuous success in biblical studies, making it hard for some to read the *Semeia* shutdown as anything less than an attempt to engineer the "end" of Theory in biblical studies (an end marked not by a bang but by a whimper: still no apocalypse, then). The rationale for the shutdown included the claim that the particularity of *Semeia* could now be adequately represented in the alleged disciplinary universalism of the *Journal of Biblical Literature*. But note our earlier caveat about Theory being used as garnish or spice to camouflage critical ingredients that may be bland or even stale.

Literary critic Valentine Cunningham misreads the menu, claiming that Theory has "spread . . . slickly" and "glibly" like a "gumbo" into such unlikely fields as geography, law, music, and even theology—by which he apparently means biblical studies, as the sole item of evidence trotted out for the Theorization of theology is the existence of *The Postmodern Bible*.[30] Cunningham has mistaken the gumbo for the main course when it is merely a side dish at most.

Litcrit asylum seekers from "Theory's Empire" like Cunningham do, however, enable us better to gauge the jaw-dropping gulf that has gradually opened up between their field and ours around the issue of Theory. We look on agog while Daphne Patai and Will H. Corral, industrious compilers of the 725-page "Anthology of Dissent" from "Theory's

---

They are *TC: A Journal of Biblical Textual Criticism* and *Online Critical Pseudepigrapha*, titles that probably tell the tale more effectively than anything we might say. The Semeia Studies monograph series, established originally as a companion to the journal, continues to be published by SBL.

30. Valentine Cunningham, "Theory, What Theory?" in Patai and Corral, *Theory's Empire*, 32: "And that's why Theory has spread so slickly, glibly even, into so many domains of the humanities—into geography (the surface of the earth is a text, and so are cities and weather systems and so on); and history (historiography is writing, ergo it's to be theorized as narrative and story and rhetoric, all tropologically, and its practitioners slotted into the gender, race, and class boxes); and music (more textual product, subject to the squeeze, of course, of race and class and gender; gender especially; can a flattened third be gay? why yes it can); and theology (the Judeo-Christian God and His Book, all easily deconstructable and narrativizable; and as for patriarchy and logocentrism, why here are their foundations); and, of course, art history (all texts); and architectural theory and practice (all texts again, and Daniel Libeskind deconstructs buildings!); and law (more text, and all deconstructable interpretative acts); and medicine (the body is a text, after all)." Cunningham's supporting endnote (40 n. 12) includes The Bible and Culture Collective, *The Postmodern Bible* (New Haven, Conn.: Yale University Press, 1995).

Empire," lament that job applicants nowadays, "ostensibly in literature," seem unable to do anything but trot out increasingly tired truisms about the "construction of national identity," "globalization," "epistemic violence," "border crossings," "transgressive sexuality," and the like.[31] We are bemused by Jonathan Culler's optimistic take on the seeming disappearance of Theory in which it becomes a "discursive space within which literary and cultural studies now occur, even if we manage to forget it, as we forget the air we breathe."[32] We marvel as Terry Eagleton bemoans the "quietly spoken middle-class students" who "huddle diligently in libraries" and work on vampirism and eye-gouging, cyberfeminism and incest, pubic hair, the literature of latex, and (most disturbing of all, no doubt) the TV sitcom *Friends*.[33]

Needless to say, such sardonic caricatures may bear as little relation to reality as the caricatures of depravity in the Prophets or the more indignant of the Catholic Epistles. Poetic or parodic license notwithstanding, however, the institutionalization of Theory within the Modern Language Association is routinely assumed even—or especially—by those most hostile to Theory. So institutionalized, indeed, has Theory become, according to Patai and Corral, that it is no longer *haute cuisine* but cafeteria fare: "more and more students these days approach theory as a tedious obligation, no longer as an exciting subject they wish to explore. In other words, theory in the classroom is, today, often little more than a routine practice, as predictable and dull as cafeteria food."[34] "Oh, no, not the gouged eyeballs again!" the hapless English Lit student might well exclaim. Once upon a time, the best and brightest of the Ivy League's literature students, among them Theorists-to-be of the stature of Gayatri Spivak and Barbara Johnson, sat at the feet of Paul de Man, Cornell and Yale professor and doyen-to-be of American deconstruction, absorbing his darkly luminous classroom pronouncements and puzzling over their meaning afterward in the corridors. These days, Ivy League students are far more prone to ironize the fashionability and revolutionary cachet of Theory, if the testimony of a Yale undergraduate writing recently in the *New York Times Magazine* is to be credited:

---

31. Patai and Corral, "Introduction," in Patai and Corral, *Theory's Empire*, 11.
32. Culler, *The Literary in Theory*, 3.
33. Eagleton, *After Theory*, 2–6.
34. Patai and Corral, "Introduction," 13.

> Lit theory is supposed to be the class where you sit at
> the back of the room with every other jaded sophomore
> wearing skinny jeans, thick-framed glasses, an ironic
> T-shirt and oversize retro headphones, just waiting for
> the lecture to be over so you can light up a Turkish Gold
> and walk to lunch while listening to Wilco. That's pretty
> much the way I spent the course, too, through structur-
> alism, formalism, gender theory, and postcolonialism.[35]

He further confesses that he was too busy shuffling through his iPod
in class to wonder what the "patriarchal world order of capitalist
oppression" had to do with *Ethan Frome*. Panning the political fervour of
what he calls "dead letter theories," he goes on to describe his discovery
of postmodernism (which he evidently believes can be disengaged from
the lifeless clutch of such theories) as a personal epiphany. The brand
of postmodernism that celebrates the ephemeral, the epiphenomenal,
and the simulacrum enabled him to understand why, for his generation,
the revolutionary aura of Theory is precisely what makes it appear
so passé. Bound up as it is with the ancient revolution of the 1960s,
Theory can now only be an ironic gesture at best, the equivalent of retro
headphones: "We are a generation for whom even revolution seems trite,
and therefore as fair a target for bland imitation as anything else. We are
the generation of the Ché Guevara T-shirt."[36] Theory thereby becomes
little more than an intellectual fashion accessory that seems quaintly,
if earnestly, out-of-date. Geriatric names like Jacques Lacan might be
replaced by slightly younger names like Slavoj Žižek, but the product
line is looking increasingly tired nonetheless.

Contrast biblical studies, in which Theory is at less risk, at least for
now, of going the way of the tie-dyed T-shirt, love beads, and the lava
lamp. Our aim in this study, however, is not to launch yet another ad
campaign to sell Theory to biblical scholars or sell them on it. The time
for that, at least, might well be past. Our intent, rather, is diagnostic
and analytic. We want to look at what has happened, what has failed to
happen, and what might yet happen in biblical studies under the heading of "Theory," and reflect on what these various "whats" reveal about

---

35. Nicholas Handler, "The Posteverything Generation," *New York Times Magazine*, September 30, 2007, 36.
36. Ibid., 43.

the very different disciplinary spaces occupied by biblical studies and literary studies, and the very different disciplinary histories that have brought each of these spaces into being. Contending that Theory's most important contribution is the self-reflexive and metacritical moves it makes possible, our reflection on Theory's reception in biblical studies is intended to defamiliarize the histories and peculiarities of our own disciplinary space.

Theory before Theory

Let's twist things around, as those (over?)-ingenious Theorists are rumored to do, and suggest an alternative and more interesting reason why biblical studies lacks protests against Theory, beyond the rather pedestrian one that it is hardly languishing at present under a surfeit of Theory. Both the demarcation of a zone called "Theory" and attempts to resist "it" or write "its" epitaph have done important work in literary studies as rallying points for disciplinary debate (not least because Theory can be so variously defined that almost any hobbyhorse can be trotted out in the case "for" or "against"). But biblical studies is such a radically different discipline that neither Theory, nor what critics are against when they declare themselves against Theory, quite translate. So different are these two disciplinary domains, in fact, that were we biblical scholars to take up the campaign against Theory in the terms in which it has been fought in literary studies, we would, as will gradually become apparent, be arguing against ourselves.

When Theory "officially" arrived on the scene in literary studies, it met itself at the door to the extent that it entered a discipline that had already taken a theoretical turn. The New Criticism that had been the dominant mode of Anglo-American literary criticism from the late 1930s onward shuttled between "practical" criticism and metacritical reflection—Theory *avant la lettre*—the latter activity steadily assuming ever-greater autonomy. By the early 1940s, Theory had begun to step out of the shadows. The word is boldly emblazoned in the title of René Wellek and Austin Warren's 1942 landmark, *Theory of Literature*.[37] William K. Wimsatt's *The Verbal Icon* from 1954, another New Critical classic, is no

---

37. René Wellek and Austin Warren, *Theory of Literature* (New York: Harcourt Brace, 1942).

less theoretical in orientation.[38] By turning New Criticism into New Theory, Yale literature professors like Wellek, Wimsatt, and Cleanth Brooks (whose *Well Wrought Urn* from 1947 also veers into Theory)[39] were unwittingly setting the stage for their usurpers, the Francophile theorists of the next generation, "some of whom were their own students."[40]

When Theory "officially" arrived on the scene in literary studies, then—and it did so most flashily at the conference that Johns Hopkins University hosted in 1966 to welcome French structuralism to America[41]—it entered a discipline that was already well-accustomed to working between literature and philosophy (in the broad, non-analytic sense), or, if you prefer, to thinking quasi-philosophically and proto-Theoretically in the ample space afforded by literature. The discipline was already replete with "abstract" reflection—enough, for example, to fill 683 pages of David Lodge's 1972 anthology, *Twentieth Century Literary Criticism*, with only a handful of those pages issuing from the French *maîtres à penser* in the person of Roland Barthes.[42] "Traditional" literary critics such as William Empson, Lionel Trilling, and Frank Kermode had been busy for decades writing on such abstract topics as ambiguity, sincerity, authenticity, time, mortality, and endings. The reading of Literature for many such critics was intimately intertwined with the task of reflecting on the human condition, albeit in an often elitist Malcolm Arnold sort of way (that was crying out for "Theoretical" demystification). It was also bound to an at once spiritualized and secularized, large and modest sense of "soul." As Theology retracted from a putative universal to a specialized preserve of the tribe called Christians and Anglo-American philosophy became more doggedly "analytic," Literature, largely a nine-

---

38. William K. Wimsatt Jr., *The Verbal Icon: Studies in the Meaning of Poetry* (Lexington: University of Kentucky Press, 1954).

39. Cleanth Brooks, *The Well Wrought Urn: Studies in the Structure of Poetry* (New York: Harcourt Brace, 1947).

40. Morris Dickstein, "The Rise and Fall of 'Practical' Criticism: From I. A. Richards to Barthes and Derrida," in Patai and Corral, *Theory's Empire*, 62.

41. In the persons of Barthes, Lacan, and Derrida (then a much lesser luminary than the other two), among others. The conference proceedings were published as Richard Macksey and Eugenio Donato, eds., *The Structuralist Controversy: The Languages of Criticism and the Sciences of Man* (Baltimore: Johns Hopkins University Press, 1970). 1966 also witnessed a thematic double issue of *Yale French Studies* (36/37) entitled "Structuralism," with articles by Lacan, Lévi-Strauss, and other early inventors of Theory.

42. David Lodge, ed., *Twentieth Century Literary Criticism: A Reader* (London: Longman, 1972).

teenth century invention, came to serve as a vital refuge for "vagrant values" such as the deviant, the erotic, the visionary, the sublime, the ineffable, and the transcendent[43]—albeit a mode of transcendence that often had a very uncomfortable, even antithetical, relationship to God(s).

What passed for normal critical practice in literary studies was, therefore, fundamentally different from its counterpart in biblical studies. The investigation of the chronological relationship between manuscripts and quartos, the quest for the identity of the "dark lady" and Shakespeare's relationship to her, the refining of textual editions, and other para-historical-critical preoccupations were but a part of critical practice. Lectures and papers about literature were frequently self-consciously performative and evangelistic. The task was to produce a piece of writing that would seduce the reader or hearer into reading or rereading Wallace Stevens or *The Yellow Wallpaper*. The labor of criticism often entailed conspicuous wordsmithery and frequently took the form of stitching different works together by means of a seemingly marginal metaphorical or thematic thread. "Strong" and idiosyncratic readings were applauded, as was overt authorship. The critic stood forth as bold critic-writer rather than self-effacing commentator hiding bashfully behind the literary text. A lecture or paper might take as its task a reflection on the paradoxical representation of truth and lying in fiction, but dealing as it did in fiction, it would have been peculiar to think of its function as a definitive exposition of the work's "truth." For literary specialists such a view would have been ripe for mockery—as it was in David Lodge's now aging but still apposite caricature of literary academia in his novel *Changing Places*. Lodge's literary-critic character Morris Zapp dreams of completing a series of commentaries on the novels of Jane Austen, "one novel at a time, saying absolutely everything that could possibly be said about them . . . so that when each commentary was written there would be simply *nothing further to say* about the novel in question"—the object, however, not being that of "enhanc[ing] others' enjoyment and understanding of Jane Austen" but of "put[ting] a definitive stop to the production of any further garbage on the subject."[44]

---

43. Cf. Eagleton, *After Theory*, 99.

44. David Lodge, *Changing Places: A Tale of Two Campuses* (London: Secker and Warburg, 1975), 34, emphasis original. Nineteenth- and early-twentieth-century biblical scholars who evoked the notion of a final commentary on a particular biblical book tended to do so without irony, as in Alfred Plummer's modest opening to his now classic Lukan commentary: "This volume has no such ambitious aim as that of being a final

It is hardly surprising that Theory found a natural habitat in such an environment. Nor is it surprising that the particular species of Theory that took root was not structuralism, with its compulsion to explain and exhaust, but deconstruction. In its early American manifestation, deconstruction was characterized by an untiring insistence on literature's sublime capacity always to exceed anything that the critic might think to say about it,[45] and as such was more of a New New Critical phenomenon than was generally realized at the time.[46] This has become ever clearer in hindsight. Typical is Rita Felski's recent observation:

> Participants in the so-called theory revolution of the last few decades often extolled the iconoclasm of their intellectual interventions, yet in practice these theories rarely if ever spawned entirely new ways of reading, but modified and fine-tuned techniques of interpretation that had been developed over decades, in some cases over centuries.
>
> We may be reminded, at this point, of the frequently made observation that deconstruction's success in the United States derived from its ability to latch on to, while burnishing with new glamour and prestige, techniques of close reading popularized during the heyday of New Criticism.[47]

---

commentary on the Gospel according to S. Luke. The day is probably still far distant when any such commentary can be written" (*A Critical and Exegetical Commentary on the Gospel According to Saint Luke* [The International Critical Commentary; Edinburgh: T. & T. Clark, 1896], iii). A far distant day, however, is different from a day whose advent is impossible in principle; and most contemporary biblical scholars understand instinctively that their discipline conspires on every level to keep the day of the final biblical commentary from ever dawning.

45. A theme first given expression by Paul de Man: "The text . . . tells the story, the allegory of its misunderstanding" (*Blindness and Insight: Essays in the Rhetoric of Contemporary Criticism* [Minneapolis: University of Minnesota Press, 1971], 136).

46. For recent adaptations of Derrida beyond earlier clichés of deconstructive practice, see, for example, the essays in Yvonne Sherwood and Kevin Hart, eds., *Derrida and Religion: Other Testaments* (London and New York: Routledge, 2005).

47. Rita Felski, "From Literary Theory to Critical Method," *Profession* (2008): 110–11. Recognition of the New New Critical character of "Yale deconstruction," in particular, is as old as Yale deconstruction itself; see especially Frank Lentricchia's scathing chapter on Paul de Man in his *After the New Criticism* (Chicago: University of Chicago Press, 1980), 282–317.

Theory glided in as, in some ways at least, a smooth extension of normal critical practice in literary studies insofar as it coupled consideration of audaciously large questions with intricate engagement with the minutiae of the words on the page.

Theory's progress, however, was uneven. It moved in with lava-like swiftness in some contexts but with glacial slowness in others. The incursions of Theory into literature departments were often gradual and belated. Outside of the charmed circle of elite departments in which the leading Theorists themselves tended to cluster, many departments were only beginning tentatively to dip their toes in Theory by the late 1980s, students being exposed to it in small (inoculating?) doses in the form of what Julian Wolfreys has termed the "Theory tourism" of the lone and detached Theory course.[48] Paul de Man's insistence that Theory has always been accompanied by a resistance to Theory is entirely apposite.[49] To that resistance we now turn.

The Inhumanity of Theory

With the arrival of Theory in literary studies as a source of regeneration and redefinition came the equally vital stimulus of Theory as that over against which to define oneself. As both welcome guest and unwelcome intruder, Theory provoked myriad performances of disciplinary redefinition or reconsolidation. But here again, just where we might expect close conjunction with biblical studies and the raising of voices essentially interchangeable with those of Barr, say, in *History and Ideology in the Old Testament* or Collins in *The Bible after Babel*, the differences are striking and instructive. The campaign against Theory in literary studies has been spearheaded by figures such as Harold Bloom, whose own early work extolled such unhistorical-critical-sounding activities as "strong misreading" and "poetic misprision"; Christopher Ricks, who writes on Bob Dylan as well as Victorian poetry and so slums it in "low" or popular culture (albeit to redeem Dylan for poetry); and Valentine Cunningham, whose *In the Reading Gaol* is a virtuoso

---

48. Julian Wolfreys, "Introduction: Border Crossings, or Close Encounters of the Textual Kind," in *Literary Theories: A Reader's Guide*, ed. Julian Wolfreys (New York: New York University Press, 1999), 1–11 passim.

49. Paul de Man, *The Resistance to Theory* (Theory and History of Literature, 33; Minneapolis: University of Minnesota Press, 1986), 3-20. Admittedly, this is a simplified take on de Man's complex argument.

performance of criticism-as-literature, with headings such as "Textual Stuff," "Handkerchief Othello," "Give me an Aposiopestic Break," and "The Wor(l)d of Mrs Woolf."[50]

Insofar as they have made common cause, campaigns against Theory have tended to unite around a soteriological, protectionist impulse: a desire to save the Author (a long-endangered species) and, by extension, the human as that which, in an ambiguously secularized world, is the source of the spiritual and the repository of meaning, all the more precious for being smaller than a god. Terry Eagleton's *After Theory*, the most visible of the anti-Theory excursions, relies heavily for its rhetorical armature on this trope of the reassertion and protection of the human. Working with a suspiciously pruned version of Theory,[51] Eagleton sets Theory up (in both senses) as that which excludes, by definition, all the truly important human stuff, like love, suffering, birth, death, ethics, and religion.

Revealingly, a large proportion of the metaphors Eagleton employs come down to differences between the human and the animal, giving his book a curiously Aesopian flavor. We are urged to retrieve the human from the clutches of Theory, red in tooth and claw, by working our way through a menagerie of fables about good and bad toads, the parochial stoat, the tiger in the bathroom, and the unusually literate zebra. Toads, it turns out, are altogether unlike human beings in that they "know by instinct how to do what it is best for toads to do. They simply follow their toad-like nature, and for them to do this is to prosper. It is to be a good toad rather than a bad one, living a fulfilling toad-like existence."[52] Like Aesop, Eagleton cannot resist hammering home the moral, in this case the distinctively human patent on morality: "Good toads are very toad-like. This is not the kind of goodness you can congratulate them on, however, since being toad-like is something they can't help being. It is not an achievement. Toads do not win medals for being toads. You can have a good toad, but not a virtuous one."[53] The truth that "we are universal animals" and "moral animals" because of "the kind of bodies

---

50. Harold Bloom, *A Map of Misreading* (Oxford: Oxford University Press, 1975); Christopher Ricks, *Dylan's Visions of Sin* (New York: Ecco, 2004); Valentine Cunningham, *In the Reading Gaol: Postmodernity, Texts and History* (Oxford: Blackwell, 1993).
51. Cf. Anderson, *The Way We Argue Now*, 1.
52. Eagleton, *After Theory*, 110.
53. Ibid.

we are born with" is reinforced by contrast with "stoats," who, it seems, are a "good deal more parochial. Because their bodies are not geared to complex production and communication, they are more restricted by their sensory experience than we are. Like village idiots and neighbourhood police officers, they are essentially local beings."[54] The moral of this fable concerns Theory, which, Eagleton asserts, is likewise local or parochial. Due to its aversion to universality, Theory is mired in the mud of locality, together with the stoat or toad.

Eagleton's moral menagerie, however, has not yet finished performing. We have yet to marvel at the "unusually literate zebra." Theory and postmodernism, for Eagleton, are characterized by a myopic moral relativism. They hold that "[t]he fact that we value Pushkin or free speech is purely contingent. We just happened to be born into the sort of set-up which admires those kinds of thing. It could easily have been otherwise."[55] The madness of this position is dramatically exposed by the "unusually literate zebra" that now trots into the ring.[56] This unthinkable thinking/writing animal could afford us a zebra-eye view of a life that was other-than-human. But seeing as there is no such thing as an unusually literate zebra, then this other-than-human view does not exist either, at least for humans.[57] Such a chimera could also undermine our belief in inalienable humanity, presumably, by demonstrating that it too can read Pushkin and espouse principles of democratic freedom. Again, however, this is impossible. Thus the unusually literate zebra consolidates, not zebraness, but humanity in all its normalcy and uniqueness.

Immensely sensitive elsewhere to the cultural constructedness of the seemingly self-evident, Eagleton ironically trots out old Aristotelian distinctions here between the human and the nonhuman. The incredulity provoked by the very notion of a thinking animal, or an animal that creates, is used to shore up our (increasingly fragile?) belief in the essential core of the "human"—and to keep us entertained in the process. For the animal with anthropomorphic pretensions is, of course, a staple of the circus. We delight to see dogs cavorting in tutus

---

54. Ibid, 157.

55. Ibid., 56.

56. As elsewhere it is exposed by the tiger in the bathroom: "All truths are established from specific viewpoints; but it does not make sense to say that there is a tiger in the bathroom from my point of view but not from yours" (ibid., 106).

57. Ibid., 55–56.

and zebras pretending to consult dictionaries. Through its metaphorical association with toads and stoats, zebras and tigers, and its seeming inability to distinguish between the human and the inhuman(e), Theory in Eagleton's *After Theory* is made the barbarian (or "village idiot") at the gates. It is placed firmly outside Literature which, like Aristotle's *polis,* becomes the primary locus for uniquely human creation and construction, and also the place where the human/humane resides and is protected. Eagleton's animal fables fall prey to one of the most recent critiques mounted by Theory and continental philosophy: the exposure of indefatigable but untenable humanisms in the modern history of philosophy and theology, including meticulous historical analyses of the construction of the human through the exclusion of the animal. Such work seeks to unravel the densely knotted connections between our anthropologies, zoologies, and theologies, and to expose the ends, edges, and limits of "man."[58] Happily oblivious to these recent evolutions in Theory, Eagleton resorts to tired dichotomies to turn Theory into the furry, slimy, low-life other of the human and the humane.

To acquire a clearer sense, however, of why Theory is currently demonized in certain circles of literary studies one needs to turn from Eagleton to other, more traditionally minded representatives of the profession. And who better to speak for the traditionalist position than the late René Wellek, principal author of the aforementioned New Critical classic *Theory of Literature,* and one of the most respected literary critics

---

58. For recent work on the human in its relations to the animal (and occasionally to the divine), see Jacques Derrida, *The Animal That Therefore I Am* (trans. David Wills; Perspectives in Continental Philosophy; New York: Fordham University Press, 2008); idem, *The Beast and the Sovereign,* vol. 1 (trans. Geoffrey Bennington; Seminars of Jacques Derrida, 1; Chicago: University of Chicago Press, 2009); Giorgio Agamben, *The Open: Man and Animal* (trans. Kevin Attell; Stanford, Calif.: Stanford University Press, 2003); Donna Haraway, *The Companion Species Manifesto: Dogs, People, and Significant Otherness* (Chicago: Prickly Paradigm, 2003); and idem, *When Species Meet* (Posthumanities; Minneapolis: University of Minnesota Press, 2007). For the larger picture, see Matthew Calarco and Peter Atterton, eds., *Animal Philosophy: Essential Readings in Continental Thought* (New York: Continuum, 2004); and Matthew Calarco, *Zoographies: The Question of the Animal from Heidegger to Derrida* (New York: Columbia University Press, 2008). For a probing theological investigation of what she calls "the fourfold of man"— that is, his raced, sexed, divine, and animal others—see Ellen T. Armour, "Touching Transcendence: Sexual Difference and Sacrality in Derrida's *Le Toucher,*" in Sherwood and Hart, *Derrida and Religion,* 351–62. Also relevant is David Wood, "Specters of Derrida: On the Way to Econstruction," in *Ecospirit: Religion, Philosophy, and the Earth,* ed. Laurel Kearns and Catherine Keller (Transdisciplinary Theological Colloquia; New York: Fordham University Press, 2007), 264–89.

of his generation. "Destroying Literary Studies" is at once the title of a 1983 article by Wellek and his answer to the question of what the more recent brand of Theory is up to:

> The day-to-day task of criticism is the sifting of the enormous production of books, and even the ranking and grading of writers. That we teach Shakespeare, Dante, or Goethe rather than the newest best-seller or any of the romances, Westerns, crime, and detective novels, science fiction, and pornography on the racks of the nearest drug store is an act of evaluation. We exercise choice the minute we take up a classical text whose value is certified by generations of readers, in deciding what features we shall pay attention to, what we shall emphasize, appreciate, and admire, or ignore and deprecate. It is now unfashionable to speak of a love of literature, of enjoyment of and admiration for a poem, a play, or a novel. But such feelings surely must have been the original stimulus to anyone engaged in the study of literature. Otherwise he might as well have studied accounting or engineering. Love, admiration, is, I agree, only the first step. Then we ask why we love and admire or detest. We reflect, analyse, and interpret; and out of this understanding grow evaluation and judgment, which need not be articulated expressly. Evaluation leads to the definition of the canon, of the classics, of the tradition. In the realm of literature the question of quality is inescapable. If this is "elitism," so be it.[59]

Wellek's jeremiad ends, somewhat poignantly, with the hope that "this new 'absurdist' wave . . . has already crashed on the shore."[60] He would live another twenty-two years, long enough to see droves of graduate students turn their back on the literature stacks of the university libraries altogether to head instead for "the racks of the nearest drug store" for material on which to write their doctoral dissertations.

---

59. René Wellek, "Destroying Literary Studies," in Patai and Corral, *Theory's Empire*, 47–48. The essay originally appeared in *The New Criterion* 2 (1983): 1–8.
60. Ibid., 51.

Lost love is a leitmotif wending its way through Daphne Patai and Will Corral's voluminous anti-Theory anthology, *Theory's Empire*. "This is what drew many of us to literature and criticism in college," one of the contributors, Morris Dickstein, reminisces. "The study of literature demanded a sheer love of language and storytelling for their own sake, yes, but the great writers also had something to say; the cognitive mysteries and affective intensities of the work of art lay before the young would-be critic like a land of dreams."[61] That the Great Authors have been displaced by the Great Theorists is what many of the contributors find hardest to swallow. "[T]he critics seem less interested in considering what literary works have to say to us than in applying a particular theory to them," John Ellis complains.[62] "And so these new professionals spiral away from anything resembling what one stubbornly continues to describe as the study of literature," adds Frank Kermode.[63] Harold Fromm goes further:

> [T]he use of literature as a weapon to fight this war against capitalism and patriarchy is all too often a violation of the creative skills and large consciousness behind the novels and poems that gives us so much psychological nourishment. . . . Works of literary genius emerge from the same human soil as everything else, and nothing is finally sacred, but reductive readings produce crabbed and crippled forms of aesthetic response, constricting rather than expanding consciousness.[64]

This elegaic lament for the tradition that extolled Great Books, Literary Masterpieces, and Authorial Genius running like a refrain through *Theory's Empire* would be unimaginable in Eagleton's *After Theory*. It dovetails neatly, nonetheless, with Eagleton's charge that Theory threatens the human. Patai and Corral summarize the sentiments of their contributors: "critics are called upon to transmit the abiding worth of literature to the coming generations. If this does not happen, our essay-

---

61. Dickstein, "The Rise and Fall of 'Practical Criticism,'" 61.
62. John Ellis, "Is Theory to Blame?" in Patai and Corral, *Theory's Empire*, 92.
63. Frank Kermode, "Changing Epochs," in Patai and Corral, *Theory's Empire*, 614.
64. Harold Fromm, "Oppositional Opposition," in Patai and Corral, *Theory's Empire*, 455.

ists fear, the humane and life-enhancing properties of literary works will be lost to us as literary studies, and literature itself, are disfigured in the distorting mirrors of the fun house of theoretical posturing."[65] Two of these essayists inquire how the avowed goal of so much Theory, which they take to be that of human emancipation, can actually be achieved by Theory, since so much of it is so unabashedly anti-humanist.[66]

The critique of Theory as anti-human(e)/anti-humanist, which is intimately bound up with the "demise of Literature" critique, is also closely tied to the third main plank of the anti-Theory platform, the identity-politics critique. "Summoning philosophical allies from Paris," Todd Gitlin protests, "the partisans of difference as a supreme principle tack together a ramshackle unity based not so much on a universalist premise or ideal as on a common enemy—the Straight White Male who, trying to obscure his power and interests, disguises himself as the human in 'humanism.' With the identity groupings, humanism is dead, a dirty word. . . ."[67] All of which (to give editors Patai and Corral the last word) brings us back once again to Literature:

> [I]dentity politics has for decades been on a collision course with the serious study of literature. Perhaps the most expressive, and most familiar, emblem of this clash is the label "Dead White Males" with which the entire Western canon (always excluding, of course, the still fashionable French *maîtres à penser*) is now routinely dismissed. The obverse of this blanket rejection is the "standpoint epistemology" that privileges, say, the writings of "women of color." The greater the claim for past oppression and marginalization, the greater the presumed validity of a group's contributions today.[68]

By defending the human(e) against Theory, Eagleton contributes to the general thrust of anti-Theory protests—at least insofar as he can:

---

65. Daphne Patai and Will H. Corral, "Introduction" (to Part VIII), in idem, *Theory's Empire*, 587.

66. Richard Freadman and Seumas Miller, "The Power and Limits of Literary Theory," in Patai and Corral, *Theory's Empire*, 78–79.

67. Todd Gitlin, "The Cant of Identity," in Patai and Corral, *Theory's Empire*, 404.

68. Daphne Patai and Will H. Corral, "Introduction" (to Part V), in idem, *Theory's Empire*, 397.

rhapsodic elegies at the graveside of the Western literary canon or bitter denunciations of minoritarian discourse are hardly within bounds for any self-respecting literary Marxist.

Theory is regularly caricatured in anti-Theory polemic as a depersonalizing force that would dissolve the human into mere textuality, or reduce literary criticism to the lowest common denominators of race-gender-class sloganeering. It is often accused of missing the meaning of literary works: not in the sense of the "one true meaning," a concept that has seldom mattered in literary criticism anyway, but the kind of meaning that Theory tends to dissolve in unsavory ideological subtexts. *Jane Eyre*, for example, must be defended against the kind of reading that would reduce it to an epiphenomenal effect of nineteenth-century imperialism, racism, and classism, or dissipate its transcendental human value in the sordid economics of the slave trade.[69]

Large sectors of the anti-Theory camp are devoted to the protection of the Author, but not in the same way that biblical scholars have sought to protect the Author. What is to be defended is not the Author as ultimate author-ity (sovereign creator of originally intended meanings, which have been unknowingly scattered and lost by pre-critical readers, and must now, as in some Gnostic myth of return, be recovered and reconstructed by critical scholars), but the Author's humanity, individuality, idiosyncrasy, creativity, and genius—all now threatened with consignment to the prison-house of language and the impersonality of semiotic systems. The self-appointed bodyguards of the Author in *Theory's Empire* like to conscript paragons of authorship such as Virginia Woolf or Margaret Atwood to the cause, seizing on authorly ripostes such as "To read on a system . . . is very apt to kill what it suits us to consider the more humane passion for pure and disinterested reading" (Woolf) and "I think I am a writer, not a sort of *tabula rasa* for the Zeitgeist or a non-existent generator of 'texts'" (Atwood).[70] The living, beat-

69. The sort of thing that Gayatri Spivak is alleged to do in her highly influential reading of *Jane Eyre*. See Gayatri Chakravorty Spivak, "Three Women's Texts and a Critique of Imperialism," *Critical Inquiry* 12 (1985): 243–61. The article (which has been reprinted in at least a dozen anthologies) begins: "It should not be possible to read nineteenth-century British literature without remembering that imperialism, understood as Britain's social mission, was a crucial part of the cultural representation of England to the English" (243).

70. Woolf's comment (from her *Hours in a Library*) appears as an epigram to Cunningham's "Theory, What Theory?" (24), while Atwood's remark (from "If You Can't Say

ing heart of authorial sensibility and creativity needs defending from poststructuralist Theories of language that would dissolve all formerly autonomous agents, not least Authors, in an acid-bath of textuality, intertextuality, semioticity, and undecidability.

Since the Author was still reflexively clutching her literary creation as she sank into the acid-bath, it too needed rescuing. One of the most common rallying-cries against Theory has been its alleged propensity to reduce literature to a "text"—a term that smacked for many of the uglification of academic prose, quasi-scientism, and the reduction of something that had once felt like a site of communion between author and reader to an object for dissection. Literature needed to be protected from Theoretical über-systems that were "cold-blooded" (to employ Eagleton's term), mechanical, reductive, and doctrinaire.[71] Often these objections emanated not just from the professorial rearguard but from students who wanted to be left alone to read without Theory intruding between them and the novel, play, or poem like a lumpish, unwelcome visitor. Nothing could be less attractive to such students than, say, the geometrical rigidity of the semiotic square. The scene of intimate, unmediated reading that they imagined was Romantic, but also reminiscent of the Reformation Protestant communing with the Word direct.[72]

Yet the campaign against Theory in literary studies, acrimonious as it has been, has produced almost no campaign buttons or stump speeches in biblical studies. Why is this? Because it doesn't translate, because there is no need for it, and because polemic against the "cold-blooded" and system- and minutiae-obsessed would have us thrusting accusing fingers in our own faces. It is hard to imagine biblical scholars uniting around a critique of the cold-blooded, since warm-bloodedness is not a criterion for membership in our discipline. The cold-blooded aberrations the anti-Theorists ascribe to Theory would merely describe business as usual in biblical studies.

For example, whereas the objectification and deconstruction of "the text" felt to many like a transgression in literary studies, it somehow

---

Something Nice Don't Say Anything At All," *Saturday Night Magazine*, 6 January 2001) is cited in Patai and Corral's "Introduction" (9). The editors deem Atwood's protest to be "emblematic of the reaction to theory of most creative writers, whose status many theorists have been eager to usurp" (ibid.).

71. Cf. Eagleton, *After Theory*, 79

72. We are, of course, talking about the Reformation ideal. In practice, unmediated communion proved deeply problematic.

seems less jarring in biblical studies.[73] The biblical text has, in effect, long been seen as an "always already" deconstructed object. This is most evident in "textual criticism" (appropriately named): its operative assumption is the ineluctable *difference* between the imperfect object present to our senses (the current edition of the *Biblia Hebraica Stuttgartensia* or the *Novum Testamentum Graece*) and the text in the putatively perfect state that the critic painstakingly seeks to reconstruct (the biblical autographs).[74] For textual criticism, that driest and dustiest of biblical disciplines and, one might imagine, farthest removed from the exotic

---

73. Assorted deconstructive forays in biblical studies can be found in the following works, among others: Robert Detweiler, ed., *Derrida and Biblical Studies* (Semeia, 23; Chico, Calif.: Scholars, 1982); Stephen D. Moore, *Literary Criticism and the Gospels: The Theoretical Challenge* (New Haven, Conn.: Yale University Press, 1989); Gary A. Phillips, ed., *Poststructural Criticism and the Bible: Text/History/Discourse* (Semeia, 51; Atlanta: Scholars, 1990); David Jobling and Stephen D. Moore, eds., *Poststructuralism as Exegesis* (Semeia, 54; Atlanta: Scholars, 1992); Stephen D. Moore, *Mark and Luke in Poststructuralist Perspectives: Jesus Begins to Write* (New Haven, Conn.: Yale University Press, 1992); idem, *Poststructuralism and the New Testament: Derrida and Foucault at the Foot of the Cross* (Minneapolis: Fortress Press, 1994); David Seeley, *Deconstructing the New Testament* (Biblical Interpretation Series, 5; Leiden: Brill, 1994); George Aichele, *Jesus Framed* (Biblical Limits; London and New York: Routledge, 1996); David Rutledge, *Reading Marginally: Feminism, Deconstruction and the Bible* (Biblical Interpretation Series, 21; Leiden: Brill, 1996); Yvonne M. Sherwood, *The Prostitute and the Prophet: Hosea's Marriage in Literary-Theoretical Perspective* (Journal for the Study of the Old Testament Supplement Series, 212; Sheffield: Sheffield Academic Press, 1996; reprinted as *The Prostitute and the Prophet: Reading Hosea in the Late Twentieth Century* [London: T. & T. Clark, 2004]); Patrick Chatelion Counet, *John, a Postmodern Gospel: Introduction to Deconstructive Exegesis Applied to the Fourth Gospel* (Biblical Interpretation Series, 44; Leiden: Brill, 2000); Robert M. Price, *Deconstructing Jesus* (Amherst, N.Y.: Prometheus, 2000); Yvonne Sherwood, ed., *Derrida's Bible: Reading a Page of Scripture with a Little Help from Derrida* (New York: Palgrave Macmillan, 2004); Theodore W. Jennings Jr., *Reading Derrida/Thinking Paul: On Justice* (Cultural Memory in the Present; Stanford, Calif.: Stanford University Press, 2005); James A. Smith, *Marks of an Apostle: Deconstruction, Philippians, and Problematizing Pauline Theology* (Semeia Studies, 53; Atlanta: Society of Biblical Literature, 2005); and Andrew P. Wilson, *Transfigured: A Derridean Rereading of the Markan Transfiguration* (Library of New Testament Studies; New York: T. & T. Clark International, 2007).

74. This is the traditional goal of textual criticism in any case, one that certain New Testament practitioners have recently been trying to shift by problematizing the quest for the autographs. See, for example, Eldon Jay Epp, *Perspectives on New Testament Textual Criticism: Collected Essays, 1962–2004* (Supplements to Novum Testamentum, 116; Leiden: Brill, 2005); Bart D. Ehrman, *Studies in the Textual Criticism of the New Testament* (New Testament Tools, Studies and Documents; Leiden: Brill, 2006); and D. C. Parker, *An Introduction to the New Testament Manuscripts and Their Texts* (Cambridge: Cambridge University Press, 2008).

excesses of Theory, the text is a para-poststructuralist object. Incurably infected with self-division, it is "at least dual."[75] It is, in fact, myriad. The original, ideal, immaterial text always floats serenely free and beyond the reach of the object-text—the text-in-fragments, that is, violently marked and marred by the history of its material transmission. Though certain of the premises of textual criticism, as traditionally conceived, are on a head-on collision course with Theory (not least around the dream of accessing origin and intention), "textuality," that Theoretical concept par excellence,[76] has certain uncanny affinities with textual criticism. Sizeable swaths of Barthes's "From Work to Text," for instance, that once celebrated manifesto for textuality, might well have been written with the bottomless waste paper basket of the biblical manuscript tradition in mind, as might his "The Death of the Author": "We know now that a text is not a line of words releasing a single 'theological' meaning (the 'message' of the Author-God), but of a multidimensional space in which a variety of writings, none of them original, blend and clash. The text is a tissue of quotations. . . ."[77] Or consider this equally well-known assertion by Derrida: "a text . . . is henceforth no longer a finished corpus of writing, some content enclosed in a book or its margins, but a differential network, a fabric of traces referring endlessly to something other than itself, to other differential traces. . . ."[78] Small wonder, then, if the concept of textuality should feel faintly familiar, at least, to biblical critics.[79] One of the first lessons that every initiate into our guild learns, after all, is that the biblical text is never simply given: it is, yet it also is not, and can never fully be.

75. To adapt a phrase from Jonathan Culler; see "Text: Its Vicissitudes," in his *The Literary in Theory*, 100.

76. "Textuality" connotes the capacity of texts to mean incessantly and uncontrollably beyond the intentions of their original authors, thereby exceeding and eclipsing their original circumstances of production.

77. Roland Barthes, "The Death of the Author," in idem, *Image—Music—Text* (trans. Stephen Heath; New York: Hill & Wang, 1987), 146. Cf. Barthes, "From Work to Text," in *Image—Music—Text*, 155–64. The essays date from 1968 and 1971 respectively.

78. Jacques Derrida, "Living On: Border Lines," in Harold Bloom et al., *Deconstruction and Criticism* (New York: Seabury, 1979), 84. For a more somber take on textuality (much of which also fits our topic, however), see Fredric Jameson, "The Ideology of the Text," in idem, *The Ideologies of Theory: Essays, 1971–1986*; Vol. 1: *Situations of Theory* (Theory and History of Literature, 49; Minneapolis: University of Minnesota Press, 1987), 17–71. Paul de Man's "The Return to Philology," in his *The Resistance to Theory*, 21–26, is also relevant.

79. Even if they feel simultaneously compelled to disavow it. See our discussion of the fate of intertextuality in biblical studies below.

Then there is our obsession with textual minutiae. We have long made our home in the kind of textual details that a traditionally minded literary critic would likely deem incidental or secondary, peripheral or tangential: the etymologies of the personal names in the Mari tablets; the probable geographical location of the land of Nod; the botanical identity of Jonah's *qiqayon* plant; fragmentary funerary texts from Ugarit; shopping lists from Oxyrhynchus; Western non-interpolations in the New Testament manuscript tradition; *hapax legomena* in the Pastoral Epistles;[80] the significance of locusts in the diet followed at Qumran—the list is infinitely long and ever more bizarre. In literary studies, meanwhile, preoccupation with the ostensibly incidental or tangential has, ironically enough, been associated not with the traditionalists in the discipline but rather with some of its least traditional—and hyper-Theoretical—practitioners, such as deconstructionists and New Historicists. The tangential obsession comes to classic expression in another oft-quoted statement by Derrida: "I do not 'concentrate,' in my reading . . . , either exclusively or primarily on those points that appear to be the most 'important,' 'central,' 'crucial.' Rather, I deconcentrate, and it is the secondary, eccentric, lateral, marginal, parasitic, borderline cases which are 'important' to me and are a source of many things, such as pleasure, but also insight into the general functioning of a textual system."[81] As biblical scholars, however, we do not need Derrida's blessing in order to dig happily with our buckets and spades in the margins of the biblical text. As Tim Beal has observed, biblical commentary and Theory share a certain "pointlessness," since both are diffused across a dizzying range of details and tangents and deconcentrate on the particular.[82] Digging in the margins has been our business and our pleasure for centuries.

In a final twist of irony, the turn to Theory for at least some of us in biblical studies actually had much to do with an attempted "humani-

---

80. Did you know that of the 848 words (excluding proper names) found in the Pastoral Epistles, 175 do not occur elsewhere in the New Testament, while an additional 306 are not in the remaining Pauline letters (even including the disputed ones), and a further 211 are part of the general vocabulary of extracanonical Christian authors of the second century?

81. Jacques Derrida, *Limited Inc* (ed. Gerald Graff; trans. Samuel Weber and Jeffrey Mehlman; Evanston, Ill.: Northwestern University Press, 1988), 44.

82. Timothy K. Beal, "Esther," in Tod Linafelt and Timothy K. Beal, *Ruth and Esther* (Berit Olam: Studies in Hebrew Narrative and Poetry; Collegeville, Minn.: Liturgical, 1999), xi.

zation" of our discipline. Our first attraction to Theory arose in part from a desire to talk about "larger human themes" in our work (even if we never used that language, even to ourselves)—themes such as bodies and embodiment, pain and pleasure, sex and death—but also more alien themes such as ecstasy and mysticism. We were drawn to overtly arational, parareligious, poststructuralist meditations and to deconstructive flirtations with negative theology—which is to say, to the tantalizingly impossible quest for transcendence in the determinedly low-ceilinged space of Theory.[83] In an interesting twist, it felt like blasphemy in biblical studies—a field that for all its theological veneer tends to aspire to "rational" and scientific modes of argumentation—to venture into the poetic and mystical regions of these religious texts.

Method Is Our Madness

It is not mysticism, however, so much as methodology that accounts for Theory's modest attractions for biblical scholars. Literary critics have been predisposed to resist the straitjacket of system and method, as we shall see, but biblical scholars have been predisposed to embrace it. Theory, insofar as it has been assimilated at all in biblical studies, has been assimilated mainly as system and method. Theory has fueled the biblical-scholarly susceptibility to methodolatry and methodone addiction. Method is our madness. Out of the ample range of options that Theory offered biblical scholars in the 1970s and 1980s, nothing was more warmly received than structuralism, semiotics, semiotic squares, actantial models, and other sharp-cornered narratological devices. The first three biblical studies journals founded as forums for methodologies other than the historical critical—*Linguistica Biblica* in Germany in 1970, *Semeia* in the United States in 1974, and *Sémiotique et Bible* in France in 1975—were founded either principally or exclusively

---

83. Deconstruction famously subjects the theological, or more properly the "metaphysical" in all its philosophical and theological guises, to stringent interrogation. Yet this blanket statement requires immediate qualification, for apophatic or negative theology, at least, has proved alluring to many deconstructors, not least Derrida himself: see especially Harold Coward and Toby Foshay, eds., *Derrida and Negative Theology* (Albany, N.Y.: State University of New York Press, 1992). Classically associated with such figures as Pseudo-Dionysius and Meister Eckhart, negative theology is a self-subverting discourse that strategically enacts its own inadequacy to the task of encapsulating the divine in human thought or language.

as forums for biblical structuralism and its closest kin: semiotics, narratology, generative poetics, sociolinguistics, and the like.

All in all, structuralism's impact on biblical studies has far exceeded its impact on literary studies, just as poststructuralism's impact on literary studies has far exceeded its impact on biblical studies. Structuralism had no sooner arrived from France than American literary critics began to tinker with it, loosen its screws, file its sharp edges, and transform it into something they soon began to call "poststructuralism"—a term that, as Derrida would wryly remark, was unknown in France until its "return" from the United States.[84] The attraction of poststructuralism, epitomized by deconstruction, was precisely that it was not structuralism, which is to say that it eschewed the structuralist project of turning literary criticism into a science by constructing ultimate explanatory models or methods that would lift the lid off literature once and for all and expose the hidden mechanisms that made it tick. Deconstruction, in contrast, was content to become "the straight-man or foil of a literary language that everywhere outwit[ted] its powers of conceptual command."[85] One of the most insistent tropes of deconstruction was the notion that the critic, while appearing to comprehend the literary text from a position securely outside or above it, is in fact being encompassed and contained by the text, enveloped within its folds, unwittingly acting out an interpretative role that the text has scripted, even dramatized, in advance.[86] In retrospect it is hardly surprising that it was poststructuralism, not structuralism, that took root and flourished in ground that had been prepared in advance by the New Critics, who themselves knew well how to genuflect before Literature. And nowhere was the unstructuralist character of poststructuralism more evident than in the assertion that early on became a mantra of American deconstruction: "Deconstruction is not a method."[87]

---

84. Jacques Derrida, "Letter to a Japanese Friend," trans. David Wood and Andrew Benjamin, in *Derrida and Différance*, ed. David Wood and Robert Bernasconi (Evanston, Ill.: Northwestern University Press, 1988), 2.

85. Richard Machin and Christopher Norris, "Introduction," in *Post-Structuralist Readings in English Poetry*, ed. Richard Machin and Christopher Norris (Cambridge: Cambridge University Press, 1987), 18.

86. This trope of the prescient text featured prominently in the work of Paul de Man, J. Hillis Miller, Barbara Johnson, and Shoshana Felman, and occasionally in the work of Derrida himself. For bibliography and further discussion, see Moore, *Mark and Luke in Poststructuralist Perspectives*, 29ff.

87. Due in no small part to Derrida's own insistence: "Deconstruction is not a method and cannot be transformed into one" ("Letter to a Japanese Friend," 3).

But deconstruction could not *not* be a method in biblical studies. Rita Felski has commented incisively on the compulsive tendency of academic disciplines to recreate elements incorporated from other disciplines in their own image and likeness:

> While literary critics, for example, are often expected to position themselves in terms of gender, race, or sexuality, scant attention is paid to disciplinary location, surely the most salient influence on how we write and read. Only when we venture abroad are we forced into a realization of the sheer contingency and strangeness of our mother tongue. Literature scholars recruited to serve on interdisciplinary hiring committees soon discover how puzzling their working assumptions can seem to scholars in other fields. These methodological differences are modified but far from dissipated by the spread of interdisciplinary work. Victorianists may pride themselves on stretching the boundaries of their field by writing on drains or Darwin, yet to outsiders their arguments, interpretations, and use of evidence unequivocally proclaim their English department training. Disciplines, in other words, are defined less by subject matter than by method.[88]

We would want to add, however, that some disciplines are more deeply defined by method than others. Specifically, we would contend that method has not meant as much for literary critics as for biblical critics. What defines the biblical studies discipline is less that it *possesses* method than that it is *obsessed with* method and as such *possessed by* method.

Biblical scholarship seems to turn everything it touches into method, even concepts as methodologically unpromising as "intertextuality." That term was coined by Julia Kristeva, as is well-known, at the heady height of Parisian (post)structuralism,[89] and exuberantly glossed by Roland Barthes, for whom the text, as intertext, was

---

88. Felski, "From Literary Theory to Critical Method," 112.
89. Julia Kristeva, "Word, Dialogue, and Novel" (French original 1969), in idem, *Desire in Language: A Semiotic Approach to Literature and Art* (trans. Leon S. Roudiez; New York: Columbia University Press, 1980), 64–91.

woven entirely with citations, references, echoes, cultural languages . . . antecedent or contemporary, which
cut across it through and through in a vast stereophony.
The intertextual in which every text is held, it itself being
the text-between of another text, is not to be confused
with some origin of the text: to try to find the "sources,"
the "influences" of a work, is to fall in with the myth of
filiation; the citations which go to make up a text are
anonymous, untraceable, and yet already read: they are
quotations without inverted commas.[90]

What happens when such a radically iconoclastic term enters the
biblical-scholarly lexicon, as it began to do in the 1980s? The unraveling
of biblical scholarship as we know it, fixated as it is on sources, influences,
and "the myth of filiation"? Not in the least. What happens for the most
part is business as usual, the ongoing preoccupation with Pentateuchal
source-paternity, inter-Isaianic textual intercourse, Synoptic *ménages à
trois*, and all the other intensely intersubjective authorial exchanges[91]
that elicit quiet excitement in the average biblical scholar—so much so
that the editor of *Intertextuality in Ugarit and Israel* is emboldened to
begin his introduction with the announcement, "To the Bible scholar,
intertextuality is nothing new,"[92] while the author of an intertextual
analysis of Matthew and Paul can remark, "It has been argued that *the
method of intertextuality*, which has been used so profitably in New
Testament scholarship, can be employed with equal benefit in a study

---

90. Roland Barthes, "From Work to Text" (French original 1971), in idem, *Image—
Music—Text*, 160.

91. Contrast Kristeva, "Word, Dialogue, and Novel," 69: "the notion of intertextuality replaces the notion of intersubjectivity. . . ." Certain of the essays collected in Danna
Nolan Fewell, ed., *Reading between Texts: The Bible and Intertextuality* (Literary Cur-
rents in Biblical Interpretation; Louisville, Ky.: Westminster John Knox, 1992) represented a different trajectory for biblical intertextuality, one less concerned with authorial
intentionality than with what exceeds and subverts it; but that has not been the version
that has caught on in biblical studies.

92. Johannes Cornelis de Moor, "Introduction," in *Intertextuality in Ugarit and
Israel: Papers Read at the Tenth Joint Meeting of The Society for Old Testament Study and
Het Oudtestamentisch Werkgezelschap in Nederland & België, Held at Oxford, 1997*, ed.
Johannes Cornelis de Moor (Leiden: Brill, 1998), ix. He continues: "The way in which
Jewish works of the Second Temple period and the New Testament used the Old Testa-
ment forced exegetes to address the issue of intertextuality long before this postmodern
shibboleth was coined" (ibid.).

of Matthew's Gospel and the Pauline epistles."[93] Richard B. Hays, one of the earliest consolidators of the method,[94] introducing the collection *Reading the Bible Intertextually*, admits: "Biblical critics are sometimes a little slow on the uptake with regard to . . . cultural fashions, but once we get wind of a new 'method,' we are sure to pursue it relentlessly for all it is worth—and maybe then some. . . . The journals are now full of essays on the intertextual analysis of everything from Genesis to Revelation, from 'Q' to the *Liber antiquitatum biblicarum* of Pseudo-Philo."[95] This proliferation, however, gives rise to a problem, namely, "that the term intertextuality is used in such diverse and imprecise ways that it becomes difficult to know what is meant by it and whether it points to anything like a method that can be applied reliably to the analysis of texts to facilitate coherent critical conversation."[96]

Faced with the domesticating capacity of such a discipline, what chance did poststructuralism in general, and deconstruction in particular, ever have of making a difference in it, much less a *différance*? The reception—or not—of deconstruction in biblical studies reveals much about the nature of the discipline. Ill-equipped to preconceive of it as anything but another method, biblical scholars immediately turned deconstruction into "deconstructionism," according it a place in the already long assembly line of critical "-isms" that lie at the center of the biblical studies enterprise: textual criticism, source criticism, tradition criticism, form criticism, redaction criticism, composition criticism, genre criticism, rhetorical criticism, feminist criticism, canonical criticism, social-scientific criticism, structuralism, narrative criticism, reader-response criticism, deconstructionism. . . . This particular "-ism" was assigned a series of spectacularly reductive definitions, along the lines of "Deconstructionism denies that texts have any single correct

---

93. David C. Sim, "Matthew and the Pauline Corpus: A Preliminary Intertextual Study," *Journal for the Study of the New Testament* 31 (2009): 418, emphasis added.

94. See Richard B. Hays, *Echoes of Scripture in the Letters of Paul* (New Haven, Conn.: Yale University Press, 1989).

95. Richard B. Hays, "Foreword to the English Edition," in *Reading the Bible Intertextually*, ed. Richard B. Hays, Stefan Alkier and Leroy A. Huizenga (Waco, Tex.: Baylor University Press, 2009), xi.

96. Ibid. The poststructuralist take on intertextuality finds token expression in the collection in George Aichele, "Canon as Intertext: Restraint or Liberation?" (*Reading the Bible Intertextually*, 139–56).

meaning or can have any single correct interpretation,"[97] which made it sound less like another useful addition to the biblical scholar's methodological toolkit than a reason for early retirement. At the same time the *word* "deconstruction(ism)," evoking esoteric procedures and complex methodological machinery, began to pop up regularly in our academic prose. The notion of advanced critical machinery for highly trained operators appealed to our biblical scholarly sensibilities. Curiosity was seldom sufficiently piqued, however, to impel one to plunge directly into the machine's manuals—Derrida's *Of Grammatology*, say, or de Man's *Allegories of Reading*—and attempt to extract the methods presumably at their core.

There was less and less method to extract from literary studies, in any case, as the 1980s gave way to the 1990s. A remarkably under-remarked feature of the four developments in literary studies that dominated the 1990s and continue to be influential down to the present—postcolonial studies, cultural studies, queer studies, and masculinity studies[98]—is that none of them offered anything much in the way of a "methodology," at least as we have been conditioned to understand that term, and cathect to it, in biblical studies.

---

97. To distil the essence of such definitions. For recent examples, see the section "Postmodernism and Deconstructionism" in Corrine L. Carvalho, *Encountering Ancient Voices: A Guide to Reading the Old Testament* (Winona, Minn.: Saint Mary's Press, 2006), 422, or the section "Postmodern Criticism" in Mark Allan Powell, "Literary Approaches and the Gospel of Matthew," in *Methods for Matthew*, ed. Mark Allan Powell (Methods in Biblical Interpretation; Cambridge: Cambridge University Press, 2009), 58–59. Colin Davis remarks of similar definitions of deconstruction in literary studies: "Why bother to read Derrida when you could rely on grotesque caricatures of his thought to rebut him?" (*After Poststructuralism*, 2–3).

98. Arguably, the only comparably high-profile development that the 2000s have yielded is ecocriticism, which, not surprisingly, is still very much in ascent. For representative work in this mode, see Cheryll Glotfelty and Harold Fromm, eds., *The Ecocriticism Reader: Landmarks in Literary Ecology* (Athens, Ga.: University of Georgia Press, 1996); Steven Rosendale, ed., *The Greening of Literary Scholarship: Literature, Theory, and the Environment* (Iowa City: University of Iowa Press, 2002); Greg Garrard, *Ecocriticism* (New Critical Idiom; London and New York: Routledge, 2004); Lawrence Buell, *The Future of Environmental Criticism: Environmental Crisis and Literary Imagination* (Blackwell Manifestos; Oxford: Wiley-Blackwell, 2005); Catrin Gersdorf and Sylvia Mayer, eds., *Nature in Literary and Cultural Studies: Transatlantic Conversations on Ecocriticism* (Nature, Culture and Literature, 3; Amsterdam and New York: Rodopi, 2006); and Helen Tiffin and Graham Huggan, *Postcolonial Ecocriticism: Literature, Animals, Environment* (London and New York: Routledge, 2010). Much of this work is deeply inflected by Theory, which sets it apart from the corresponding corpus of work in biblical studies, typified by the five-volume Earth Bible series (Sheffield: Sheffield Academic;

British cultural studies did develop certain distinctive methodological procedures during the 1970s and early 1980s.[99] By the time cultural studies began to take the U.S. academy by storm in the late 1980s and early 1990s, however, it had all but uncoupled itself from method as such. What was distinctive (and controversial) about U.S. cultural studies was its preferred objects of analysis, as we shall see, not its analytical procedures.[100] What of postcolonial studies? Despite the colossal critical literature that the field has spawned, it has yielded remarkably little in the way of readily identifiable methodologies or even general strategies of reading. What does immediately leap to mind are the immensely influential concepts set forth (in thoroughly unsystematic fashion) by Homi Bhabha in certain of his early essays on nineteenth-century India collected in *The Location of Culture*—colonial ambivalence, mimicry, and hybridity.[101] These three interrelated concepts do provide a productive reading grid that can readily, if not unproblematically, be superimposed on texts emerging from empire, including biblical texts.[102]

Cleveland: Pilgrim, 2000–2002). A thriving subfield of ecocriticism centres on human-animal relations, and has been dubbed "animal studies," "animality studies," or "posthuman animality studies." For an excellent overview, see Cary Wolfe, "Human, All Too Human: 'Animal Studies' and the Humanities," *PMLA* 124 (2009): 564–75. This subfield receives its primary impetus, at least within the field of literary studies, from certain animal books written by leading Theorists (see the works listed in n. 59 above).

99. As briefly outlined in Stephen D. Moore, "Between Birmingham and Jerusalem: Cultural Studies and Biblical Studies," *Semeia* 82 (1998): 7–8.

100. A lack (if that indeed is what it is) that James Schwoch, Mimi White, and Dilip Gaonkar, eds., *The Question of Method in Cultural Studies* (Oxford: Blackwell, 2005) attempts to redress. The thing to be noted for our purposes, however, is that the volume emerges out of a general perception that the question of method in cultural studies is a puzzling and vexing one.

101. See Homi K. Bhabha, *The Location of Culture* (London and New York: Routledge, 1994).

102. See, for example, Tat-siong Benny Liew, *Politics of Parousia: Reading Mark Inter(con)textually* (Biblical Interpretation Series, 42; Leiden: Brill, 1999); Erin Runions, *Changing Subjects: Gender, Nation and Future in Micah* (Playing the Texts, 7; Sheffield: Sheffield Academic, 2002); Jin Hee Han, "Homi Bhabha and the Mixed Blessings of Hybridity in Biblical Hermeneutics," *The Bible and Critical Theory* 1 (2005): http://publications.epress.monash.edu/loi/bc; Yong-Sung Ahn, *The Reign of God and Rome in Luke's Passion Narrative: An East Asian Global Perspective* (Biblical Interpretation Series, 80; Leiden: Brill, 2006); Stephen D. Moore, *Empire and Apocalypse: Postcolonialism and the New Testament* (The Bible in the Modern World, 12; Sheffield: Sheffield Phoenix, 2006); Robert Paul Seesengood, *Competing Identities: The Athlete and the Gladiator in Early Christianity* (Library of New Testament Studies, 346; New York: T. & T. Clark International, 2006); Simon Samuel, *A Postcolonial Reading of Mark's Story of Jesus* (Library of New Testament Studies; New York: T. & T. Clark International, 2007); and for

Gayatri Spivak's no less influential oeuvre, however, offers exceedingly slim pickings for the method-hungry biblical critic,[103] as, indeed, does Edward Said's, the latter arguably yielding only the sweepingly general strategy of "contrapuntal reading."[104]

Queer studies and masculinity studies, too, along with autobiographical criticism (a more fleeting but also influential product of the 1990s), offer extremely little in the way of repeatable methodological procedures.[105] They seem to offer nothing comparable even to Derrida's early (and, for many years, endlessly cited) description of deconstruction as an operation conducted in two successive phases, "reversal" and

---

incisive critique of Bhabha, Joseph A. Marchal, *The Politics of Heaven: Women, Gender, and Empire in the Study of Paul* (Paul in Critical Contexts; Minneapolis: Fortress Press, 2008).

103. Although one can do a surprising amount with a few scraps; see especially Laura E. Donaldson, "Gospel Hauntings: The Postcolonial Demons of New Testament Criticism," in *Postcolonial Biblical Criticism: Interdisciplinary Intersections*, ed. Stephen D. Moore and Fernando F. Segovia (The Bible and Postcolonialism, 8; New York: T. & T. Clark International, 2005), 97–113; and Tat-siong Benny Liew, "Postcolonial Criticism: Echoes of a Subaltern's Contribution and Exclusion," in *Mark and Method: New Approaches in Biblical Studies*, ed. Janice Capel Anderson and Stephen D. Moore (2nd ed.; Minneapolis: Fortress Press, 2008), 211–31. Then again, what would constitute a famine for many biblical critics constitutes a feast for many literary critics: "A Spivakian methodology hinges on the following: acknowledging complicity, learning to learn from below, unlearning one's privilege as loss, working without guarantees, persistently critiquing the structures that one inhabits intimately and that one cannot say no to, and giving attention to subject formation such that it 'produc[es] the reflexive basis for self-conscious social agency.'" Sangeeta Ray, "An Ethics on the Run," *PMLA* 123 (2008): 238, quoting Spivak, "Not Really a Properly Intellectual Response: An Interview with Gayatri Spivak" (conducted by Tani E. Barlow), *Positions* 12 (2004): 153.

104. On which see Edward W. Said, *Culture and Imperialism* (New York: Vintage, 1993), especially 51, 66–67.

105. Queer theory, the most visible manifestation of queer studies, is a quintessentially poststructuralist "take" on sex and sexual identity that argues their constructedness and fluidity. Masculinity studies, though less intimately intertwined with poststructuralism, also tends to be thoroughly constructionist in its approach to gender. See further Iain Morland and Annabelle Willox, eds., *Queer Theory* (Readers in Cultural Criticism; New York: Palgrave Macmillan, 2005); Lynne Huffer, *Mad for Foucault: Rethinking the Foundations of Queer Theory* (Gender and Culture; New York: Columbia University Press, 2009); Tim Edwards, *Cultures of Masculinity* (London and New York: Routledge, 2006); Todd W. Reeser, *Masculinities in Theory: An Introduction* (Oxford: Wiley-Blackwell, 2010). For biblical work informed by queer theory, see Stephen D. Moore, *God's Beauty Parlor: And Other Queer Spaces in and Around the Bible* (Contraversions: Jews and Other Differences; Stanford, Calif.: Stanford University Press, 2001); Ken Stone, *Practicing Safer Texts: Food, Sex and Bible in Queer Perspective* (Queering Theology; New York: T. & T. Clark International, 2004); and certain of the contributions to Ken Stone, ed., *Queer Commentary and the Hebrew Bible* (Journal for the Study of the

"reinscription";[106] or of Aram Veeser's encapsulation of New Historicism (at least as practiced by its preeminent exponent, Stephen Greenblatt) as an analytic strategy that typically moves through five successive "moments": anecdote, outrage, resistance, containment, and autobiography.[107] Queer studies and masculinity studies do effect a radical reframing of sex, sexuality, and/or gender that draws the critic's eye compulsively to certain features of a text and even predetermines the broad contours of a reading. But each of these developments, along with postcolonial studies and cultural studies, seem to have more in common methodologically with feminist studies, say, than with form criticism, redaction criticism, rhetorical criticism, structuralism, narrative criticism, or any of the other major "-isms" in biblical studies. In literary studies, as in biblical studies, feminist criticism has not been associated with any one methodology. Rather it has been a radically eclectic enterprise, methodologically speaking. What feminist scholars do share in common is a critical sensibility, an encompassing angle of vision that, in a more fundamental fashion than a methodological framework, brings previously unperceived or disavowed data into focus.[108] And postcolonial studies, cultural studies, queer studies, and masculinity studies seem to operate similarly.[109] Autobiographical criticism, for its part (a more fleeting but nonetheless influential product of the same era), also diverges strikingly from traditional methodology, the critic's personal history forming the explicit reading frame into which the text is placed and in relation to which it assumes fresh meaning.[110]

Old Testament Supplement Series, 334; Sheffield: Sheffield Academic, 2001), and Deryn Guest, Robert E. Goss, Mona West, and Thomas Bohache, eds., *The Queer Bible Commentary* (London: SCM, 2006). For masculinity studies as biblical studies, see Stephen D. Moore and Janice Capel Anderson, eds., *New Testament Masculinities* (Semeia Studies, 45; Atlanta: Society of Biblical Literature, 2003); Colleen M. Conway, *Behold the Man: Jesus and Greco-Roman Masculinity* (Oxford: Oxford University Press, 2008); and Ovidiu Creangă, ed., *Men and Masculinity in the Hebrew Bible and Beyond* (Sheffield: Sheffield Phoenix, 2010). Autobiographical criticism is discussed below.

106. Jacques Derrida, *Positions* (trans. Alan Bass; Chicago: University of Chicago Press, 1981 [French original 1972]), 41–43.

107. H. Aram Veeser, "The New Historicism," in *The New Historicism Reader*, ed. H. Aram Veeser (London and New York: Routledge, 1993), 5.

108. Cf. Mary Margaret Fonow and Judith A. Cook, eds., *Beyond Methodology: Feminist Scholarship as Lived Research* (Bloomington: University of Indiana Press, 1991).

109. Cultural studies is discussed in more detail below.

110. See Diane P. Freedman, Olivia Frey, and Frances Murphy Zauhar, eds., *The Intimate Critique: Autobiographical Literary Criticism* (Durham, N.C.: Duke University Press,

This post-methodological swerve in literary studies (effected unself-consciously, it would seem, with no manifestos to herald it) offers an instructive contrast to the established modes of reading in biblical studies. For methodology has long been the *sine qua non* of biblical studies as an academic discipline.[111] Methodology is what is meant to keep our discourse on the Bible from being subjective, personal, private, pietistic, pastoral, devotional, or homiletical. Methodology is what is meant to maintain the dividing partition between sermon and scholarship, and prevent the lecturer's podium from morphing into a pulpit. The homily has long been the constitutive other of biblical criticism, in other words, and methodology the enabling condition of such criticism—"methodology" here being a cipher for "objectivity," "neutrality," "disinterestedness," and all of the other related and foundational values of biblical studies as an academic discipline. These values are rarely trumpeted nowadays, at least in Anglophone biblical scholarship (evidence of the impact of postmodernism on the field), but continue to hold sway, seemingly, over most practitioners of the discipline anyway, at least to the extent that scholars resist seeing their own scholarship as advocacy for the interests of their class or any other—that being the perceived preserve of other (less scholarly) scholars who wear their political agenda on their sleeve. (That perception is evidence of the lack of impact of postmodernism on the field.)[112]

But our quarantining of the biblical-critical from the homiletical has not occurred without cost. Most obviously, our obsession with method has made for a mountainous excess of dull and dreary books, essays,

---

1993); and Diane P. Freedman and Olivia Frey, eds., *Autobiographical Writings Across the Disciplines: A Reader* (Durham, N.C.: Duke University Press, 2003). For autobiographical criticism in biblical studies, see Janice Capel Anderson and Jeffrey L. Staley, eds., *Taking It Personally: Autobiographical Biblical Criticism* (Semeia, 72; Atlanta: Scholars, 1995); Jeffrey L. Staley, *Reading with a Passion: Rhetoric, Autobiography, and the American West in the Gospel of John* (New York: Continuum, 1995); Ingrid Rosa Kitzberger, ed., *The Personal Voice in Biblical Interpretation* (London and New York: Routledge, 1998); idem, ed., *Autobiographical Biblical Criticism: Between Text and Reader* (Leiden: Deo, 2002); and Fiona C. Black, ed., *The Recycled Bible: Autobiographical Criticism, Cultural Studies, and the Space Between* (Semeia Studies, 51; Atlanta: Society of Biblical Literature, 2006).

111. More precisely, since the Enlightenment, as we shall see.

112. Homiletics, too, of course, is a field much preoccupied with method. It seems to us, however, that methodology plays a substantially different role in homiletics than in traditional biblical scholarship. To put it mildly, the function of method in homiletics is hardly that of facilitating a disinterested stance on the part of interpreter and audience toward the biblical text.

and articles: here, first, in numbing dry detail is my method; now watch and be amazed while I apply it woodenly to this unsuspecting biblical text. In addition, the restless quest for ever-new methods with which to read the same old texts has always predetermined our dealings as biblical scholars with literary studies. Even celebrations of readerly subjectivity and autonomy in literary studies, or impassioned cries for freedom from the straitjackets of Theory and methodology, have quickly congealed into still further methods as soon as they came into contact with biblical studies, as we shall see. Meanwhile, important historiographical developments in literary studies have gone largely unnoticed in biblical studies, even, or especially, by historical critics.

Unhistorical Criticism

In a move that was at once inevitable and unfortunate, Theory as it entered biblical studies was stamped quite specifically as *Literary* Theory, campaigning for freedom from *History's* Empire. The original wagon train setting off into the sunset of Theory was packed with self-proclaimed dissidents, discontents, refugees, and asylum seekers from the totalitarian state of historical criticism, demanding the right to do something, anything, else—and the overdetermined heading of (Literary) Theory came to stand for that anything, and everything, else. The advent of Theory in biblical studies was caught up in the dichotomy of the literary and the historical, or in much-loved terms that smacked reassuringly of scientific specialization, the "synchronic" and the "diachronic." The dichotomization of Theory and historiography was inevitable, given historical criticism's monopoly of the field, but it also served to ensure from the outset that Theory's impact on the field would be minimal. To invite the accusation or even the suspicion that one's work was "ahistorical" was to put oneself beyond the pale of "serious" biblical scholarship and beyond the kinds of questions that the guild was predisposed to recognize as the ones that really mattered. That is why tirades against Theory have been few and far between in biblical studies— Theory has had too little impact, all told, to merit much attention—while the confrontation between historical "minimalism" and "maximalism" is frequently the occasion for sell-out duels with pistols at dawn.

Ironically, however, even as the wagon train of Theorists was trundling out of historical-critical territory in biblical studies, literary Theorists were busy rediscovering history. In reaction to the perceived ahistorical formalism of early American deconstruction (epitomized by the work of Paul de Man and J. Hillis Miller), Theory in literary studies began to take a sharp historiographical turn. Driving this development were such field-reorienting phenomena as colonial discourse analysis (later to be relabelled postcolonial theory) and New Historicism.[113] New "historicisms" replaced old "formalisms," and "formalism" became a term of abuse in literary circles.[114] Had biblical literary criticism, in its first youthful flush of attraction to Theory, been more attuned to and more taken with these poststructuralist experiments in historiography, what difference, if any, might it have made for Theory's reception and dissemination in biblical studies?[115] We can only speculate.

Yet it is not as though the fixation with history characteristic of biblical scholarship had no effect whatsoever on biblical literary critics, even those ostensibly in flight from historical criticism. For the importation

---

113. Edward Said's *Orientalism* (New York: Vintage, 1978) came to be seen retrospectively as the charter document of colonial discourse analysis (and then of postcolonial theory), while Stephen Greenblatt's *Renaissance Self-Fashioning: From More to Shakespeare* (Chicago: University of Chicago Press, 1980) came to be seen as the seminal text of New Historicism (even though Greenblatt did not coin the term until 1982). For an excellent introduction to New Historicism, see Catherine Gallagher and Stephen Greenblatt, *Practicing New Historicism* (Chicago: University of Chicago Press, 2000), together with Veeser, *The New Historicism Reader*.

114. More recently, the very concept of formalism has been problematized, certain critics arguing that it was in fact, and of necessity, always covertly attached to histories, contexts, authors, and referents. See, for example, Culler, *The Literary in Theory*, 9–12, 99–116, esp. 101–3; Butler, Guillory and Thomas, "Preface," in idem, *What's Left of Theory?* viii–x. Culler argues that "the text itself" was always a "complicated positivity," even for the New Critics (102), while Butler, Guillory, and Thomas argue that deconstruction entailed the following complexification of New Critical formalism: "There is always that which calls the form into question, and that is not simply another formal element, but a resistant remainder that sets limits to formalism itself" (ix).

115. Biblical studies engagement with New Historicism, in particular, has been slight and sporadic. See Lori L. Rowlett, *Joshua and the Rhetoric of Violence: A New Historicist Analysis* (Journal for the Study of the Old Testament Supplement Series, 226; Sheffield: Sheffield Academic, 1996); Stephen D. Moore, ed., "The New Historicism," *Biblical Interpretation* 5:4, 1997 (thematic issue); Gina Hens-Piazza, *The New Historicism* (Guides to Biblical Scholarship; Minneapolis: Fortress Press, 2002); Colleen M. Conway, "The Production of the Johannine Community: A New Historicist Approach," *Journal of Biblical Literature* 121 (2002): 479–95; idem, "The New Historicism and the Historical Jesus in John: Friends or Foe?" in *John, Jesus, and History*; Vol. 1: *Critical Appraisals of Critical Views*, ed. Paul N. Anderson, Felix Just, S.J., and Tom Thatcher (Society of Biblical Literature Symposium Series, 44; Leiden: Brill, 2007), 199–216; and idem, "Supplying the Missing Body of Onesimus: Readings of Paul's Letter to Philemon," in *Sacred Tropes: Tanakh, New Testament, and Qur'an as Literature and Culture*, ed. Roberta Sterman Sabbath (Biblical Interpretation 98; Leiden: Brill, 2009), 475–84.

of Theory into biblical studies soon led to an almost obsessive concern with the author, tethered as he was to history, and his troubled relationship with the reader. Reader-oriented Theory, in particular, quickly morphed into a debate about the power of the historical author, abetted by his intratextual henchman the implied author, relative to that of the reader in their perpetual tug-of-war over the text's meaning, a tussle in which the reader could only ever be on the losing side, given the biblical scholar's fixation on authorial intentions. No works of reader-response criticism were more warmly received by biblical scholars than Wolfgang Iser's *The Implied Reader* and *The Act of Reading*, notwithstanding the fact that they were repeatedly panned by secular literary critics for seeming to offer the reader a bill of emancipation from the author with one hand while surreptitiously tearing it up with the other.[116] To this day, meanwhile, no major works of reader-response criticism have received less attention from biblical reader-response critics than David Bleich's *Subjective Criticism*, Norman Holland's *5 Readers Reading*, and other work similarly focused on the unpredictable meanderings of "real" readers as opposed to the lockstep goose-stepping of "ideal" readers.[117] Real readers did not fit well into the machinery of method. We were much more comfortable with readerly cyborgs—ideal readers, intended readers, model readers, inscribed readers, encoded readers, implied readers, informed readers, competent readers, narratees, readers-in-the-text—who had been programed by historical authors to read in rigidly predetermined ways. More precisely, we ourselves had been programed by our disciplinary formation to read in these mechanical ways. But what were the historical and cultural forces that had formed the discipline itself? How do we account for the ineluctable strangeness of the biblical scholar? To those questions we now turn.

---

116. Wolfgang Iser, *The Implied Reader: Patterns of Communication in Prose Fiction from Bunyan to Beckett* (Baltimore: Johns Hopkins University Press, 1974), and idem, *The Act of Reading: A Theory of Aesthetic Response* (Baltimore: Johns Hopkins University Press, 1978). For discussion of Iser's practice of granting the implied reader freedom in theory only to withdraw it in the actual interpretation of literary works, see Moore, *Literary Criticism and the Gospels*, 100–7 passim.

117. David Bleich, *Subjective Criticism* (Baltimore: Johns Hopkins University Press, 1978); Norman N. Holland, *5 Readers Reading* (New Haven, Conn.: Yale University Press, 1975). For more recent attempts to complicate overly generic and idealized "reader constructs," see the essays collected in Elizabeth A. Flynn and Patrocinio P. Schweickart, eds., *Reading Sites: Social Difference and Reader Response* (New York: Modern Language Association of America, 2004).

What is written here must not be read as though
intended for Scriptural exegesis, which lies beyond
the limits of the domain of bare reason. It is possible to explain how an historical account is to be put
to a moral use without deciding whether this is the
intention of the author or merely our interpretation,
provided this meaning is true in itself, apart from all
historical proof, and is moreover the only one whereby
we can derive something conducive to our betterment
from a passage which otherwise would only be an
unfruitful addition to our historical knowledge.[1]

The sentimental feelings we all have for those things
we were educated to believe sacred, do not readily
yield to pure reason. I distinctly remember the shud-
der that passed over me on seeing a mother take our
family Bible to make a high seat for her child at table.
It seemed such a desecration. I was tempted to protest
against its use for such a purpose, and this, too, long
after my reason had repudiated its divine authority.[2]

THE
INVENTION
OF THE
BIBLICAL
SCHOLAR

The Epistemic Abyss

The differences between biblical critics and literary critics that we have been pondering do not come down to talent, temperament, or individual choice. Our argument is not that biblical critics are genetically "cold-blooded" and reptilian[3] or particularly prone to methodone dependency. The differences are rather a product of the history, contours, and constraints of our particular disciplinary space, which is also a social and cultural space. And it is in relation to these inherited disciplinary traits that our disciplinary response to Theory (so far as it can be spoken of in the singular) is best situated and understood.

Michel Foucault, in his early High-Theoretical opus *Les Mots et les choses*, famously argued that history does not unfold smoothly, inexorably, or organically along causal lines of continuity but rather by way of jagged, jerky, discontinuous leaps that he dubbed "epistemic breaks."[4] *Epistémè* (loosely translatable as "knowledge") was Foucault's term for the labyrinthine totality of a priori, largely unconscious, and largely unwritten prescriptions, proscriptions, and assumptions that regulate the production of knowledge in a given historical epoch, and hence enable the finite set of statements that are acceptable in that epoch ("factual" statements, for instance) to stand out from the infinite set of statements that are merely possible.[5] According to Foucault, however, one era's *epistémè* does not contain, tidily concealed within its folds, the

---

1. Immanuel Kant, *Religion within the Limits of Reason Alone* (trans. with introduction by Theodore M. Greene and Hoyt H. Hudson; Chicago and London: Open Court, 1934 [German original 1793]), 39.

2. Elizabeth Cady Stanton, "Introduction," in idem et al., *The Woman's Bible* (New York: European Publishing Company, 1895), vol. 1, 11–12.

3. Cf. Terry Eagleton, *After Theory* (New York: Basic, 2003), 79, as discussed above.

4. *Coupures épistémologique*, a term Foucault adapted from Gaston Bachelard. The term and/or concept features prominently in at least three of Foucault's early books, but with minor semantic shifts that need not concern us here. See Michel Foucault, *The Order of Things: An Archaeology of the Human Sciences* (New York: Pantheon, 1970; anonymous trans. of *Les Mots et les choses: Une archéologie des sciences humaines*, 1966), *The Archaeology of Knowledge* (New York: Pantheon, 1972; trans. by Alan Sheridan of *L'Archéologie du savoir*, 1969), and *The Birth of the Clinic: An Archaeology of Medical Perception* (New York: Pantheon, 1973; trans. by Alan Sheridan of *Naissance de la clinique: Une archéologie du regard medical*, 1963).

5. Cf. Michel Foucault, "The Confession of the Flesh," in idem, *Power/Knowledge: Selected Interviews and Other Writings, 1972-1977* (ed. Colin Gordon; New York: Pantheon, 1980), 197.

épistémè of the succeeding era; hence his concept of the epistemic break or rupture.

The history of biblical interpretation in the early modern period arguably offers a more compelling illustration of the epistemic break than any that Foucault himself is able to marshal in *Les Mots et les choses* or his subsequent work. At issue is the radical disjunction and discontinuity between certain unprecedented eighteenth-century responses to the Bible on the one hand, and all the modes of Christian biblical interpretation that preceded them on the other hand. It is not too hard to imagine that Origen and Augustine, Abelard and Aquinas, Luther and Calvin, for all their significant differences, could nevertheless have conducted a relatively civil and fairly profitable seminar on the biblical text and its proper interpretation.[6] The essential and enabling rule for biblical scholarship from the second-century apologists down to the sixteenth-century Reformers was the rule of faith; it was that rule— actually a complex congeries of minute regulations and encompassing assumptions—that determined the enterprise of biblical scholarship down to its details, however much those details might shift, slide, disintegrate, and reform in the ceaseless ebb and flow of the historical tide. Beginning in the late seventeenth century, however, and intensifying in the eighteenth, with epistemic fault lines raising, then closing, the question of the *immorality* of the biblical text emerged, and put a nascent and self-conscious domain known as biblical scholarship into a defensive and exclusive relationship with history.

Whence this epistemic upheaval? In response to the unprecedented threat to biblical authority intrinsic to Enlightened modernity, Enlightenment and post-Enlightenment defenders of the Bible forged what historian Jonathan Sheehan has termed "the Cultural Bible" or "the Enlightenment Bible"—a model of biblical authority that could withstand the extreme pressures of a post-theological era.[7] Theological

---

6. Cf. Gerald Bray, *Biblical Interpretation: Past and Present* (Downers Grove, Ill.: InterVarsity, 1996), 250–51: "Jerome, Andrew of St. Victor and Calvin would have been at home with each other—speaking the same language, reading the same classics and honouring the same methods of study. We might choose to call one tradition 'Antiochene' and the other 'Alexandrian,' but these labels mean less than we might think. In spite of the many differences, there was one world, one mental universe, which forty generations of Christians had shared."

7. Jonathan Sheehan, *The Enlightenment Bible: Translation, Scholarship, Culture* (Princeton, N.J.: Princeton University Press, 2004), xi. "Enlightenment," as Sheehan

authority was translated into cultural authority. If the answer to the question "Why should I read the Bible?" had previously been "because it reveals the means to your salvation," the Enlightenment Bible supplied a series of supplemental, even alternative, answers, meeting the challenge to the Bible's authority by dispersing that authority across different domains.[8] The Bible was rehabilitated on primarily (if ambiguously) human terms, as the foundation of culture and hence a legitimate object of cultural inquiry. The primary location of these efforts was Germany, where "the philological sciences teamed up most effectively and explicitly with the zealous efforts of religious reformers to keep the Bible fresh and relevant to the modern age."[9] In the mid- to late eighteenth century, biblical scholarship was established as the space in which this task of extending and sustaining the relevance of the Bible—now positioned under a Damoclean sword of potential irrelevance for the first time in its history—would take place.

Our argument in this book is that contemporary biblical scholarship, including even those developments within it that most readily invite the label "postmodern(ist)," is still fundamentally predetermined and contained by the Enlightenment *épistémè*, and far more than is generally realized. The Bible of contemporary biblical scholarship remains the Enlightenment Bible. Despite the alleged "fragmentation" of the historical-critical paradigm associated with the recent multiplication of methods and the intensification of interdisciplinarity in biblical studies, we contend that no fundamental rupture of the biblical-scholarly *épistémè* has yet occurred remotely comparable to that which brought the discipline into being in the first place. This is not to suggest, however, that the history of critical biblical scholarship should, therefore, be seen as a smoothly unfolding saga, devoid of discontinuities and disjunctions. The temptation to compose histories of biblical criticism as aetiological sagas, implicitly designed to demonstrate how all the essential elements of contemporary historical-critical method are present in embryo in eighteenth- and nineteenth-century biblical scholarship, has been considerable. What even an account of nascent biblical criticism

---

defines the term, denotes a "constellation of practices and institutions" developed or refined in the eighteenth century "to address the host of religious, historical, and philosophical questions inherited from the Renaissance, the Reformation, and the Scientific Revolution" (ibid., xi–xii).

8. Ibid., xii.

9. Ibid., xiii.

as original and insightful as Sheehan's *The Enlightenment Bible* fails to register, in particular, is a significant, indeed symptomatic, disjunction between eighteenth- and nineteenth-century biblical criticism around the issue of morality.

The Invention of "Moral Unbelief"

Histories of biblical criticism ordinarily represent the problem of the Bible's historicity as beginning to register inescapably and programmatically for biblical scholars during the prolonged moment in early modern European culture loosely known as "the Enlightenment." What standard histories of the discipline tend not to emphasize, in contrast, is the extent to which the *morality* of the Bible emerged as a prior and larger problem during this period.[10] What might be termed the "first wave" of Enlightenment challenge to the Bible called the integrity of the biblical authors into question in various senses: whether they were trustworthy in what they said or whether they were lying, and whether they were who they said they were. The question of the integrity of the text—which was to become the sole obsession of later historical critics— was originally raised as a subsection of the larger question of integrity in general.

Early modern Europeans, engaging with the Bible as a social, political, and theological force and cultural exemplar, were concerned, above all, with questions of what Kant termed moral faith and, conversely, *moral unbelief.* Moral unbelief became possible when morality was deemed to have sources other than, or in addition to, the Bible, and

---

10. When the more detailed of these histories do deal with eighteenth-century moral critique of the Bible, such treatment tends to be strictly teleological, the significance of such critique being measured mainly by the extent to which it succeeds in anticipating the historical-critical method. William Baird's discussion of the "The Attack on Revealed Religion: The English Deists" in the first volume of his massive *History of New Testament Research* (vol. 1: *From Deism to Tübingen* [Minneapolis: Fortress Press, 1992], 31–57) is typical in this regard. Of Thomas Morgan, for instance, an eighteenth-century thinker who will feature prominently in our own account, Baird at one point remarks: "In the course of the dialogue, Morgan engages in biblical criticism. He argues that the Scriptures should be interpreted historically . . ." (53). Our point is that early biblical criticism needs to be reconceived more broadly. Similarly, of Thomas Chubb, another important figure for us, Baird writes: "In studying the Bible, Chubb offers a bold venture into historical-critical method . . ." (54). It is precisely when such early biblical scholars are performing something radically other than the analytic strategy that later congealed as historical criticism that they are of most interest to us.

the Bible viewed in light of these sources appeared, in part at least, to be morally dangerous or regressive. At such points, many eighteenth-century intellectuals reasoned, readers were under an *obligation* to criticize the Bible. Blurring the two questions of historical plausibility and moral efficacy and *giving priority to the latter*, Kant argues that those who maintain "if it is untrue . . . I have merely believed it superfluously" are guilty of a "violation of conscience."[11] He does not mean that believing in incredible events, such as the parting of the Red Sea or Moses detailing his own death, with one's fingers crossed involves a violation of conscience, but such events are only the "parerga" or superfluities of true religion. What really matters is the moral core, or, more precisely, the divinity of the Bible's moral content: "The divinity of [the Bible's] moral content adequately compensates reason for the humanity of [the Bible's] historical narrative which, like an old parchment that is illegible in places, has to be made intelligible by adjustments and conjectures consistent with the whole."[12] Whereas earlier exegetes manipulated and moralized the Bible behind the scenes, the modern philosopher must be explicit about criticizing aspects of the Bible's letter in the name of the spirit, or the moral core (cf. 2 Cor. 3). He must openly articulate the textual sore spots and potential sites of moral unbelief.

Far from being unique, Kant's formulation was the culmination of certain tense and explicit renegotiations between the Bible and morality that had been taking place, publicly in print, since at least the late seventeenth century. This debate on biblical error orbited obsessively around such iconic biblical crimes as the divinely mandated genocide of the Canaanites, Abraham's willingness to offer Isaac as a bloody sacrifice, and the manifest moral sins of David, the "man after [God's] own heart" (Acts 13:22). Pierre Bayle (1647–1706), in the first uncensored version of his article on David in his hugely influential *Dictionnaire historique et critique*, commented wryly on Saul's odd amnesia in the Goliath episode:

> It is a little strange that Saul did not know David, since the young man had several times played on instruments of

---

11. Kant, *Religion within the Limits of Reason Alone*, 176–77.

12. Immanuel Kant, *The Conflict of the Faculties/Der Streit der Fakultäten* (trans. Mary J. Gregor; Lincoln: University of Nebraska Press, 1979 [German original 1798]), 117–19.

music in his presence, to calm the dismal vapours which
disturbed him. If such a relation were found in Thucy-
dides or Livy, all the critics would unanimously conclude
that the transcribers had transposed the pages, forgotten
something in one place, repeated something in another,
or inserted additional passages in the Author's Work.[13]

But just as Kant could forgive the "humanity of the Bible's historical
narrative" but not the inhumanity or immorality that detracted from
its moral core, so Bayle regarded the Bible's technical errors as a
mere sideshow to David's manifest immorality. Deeming the Bible's
enumeration of David's crimes as too conservative at only one (cf. 2
Sam. 11:27: "But the thing that David had done displeased the Lord"),
Bayle came to a more generous total. Numerous other victims, including
Saul and the neighboring tribes, had joined the ghost of Uriah in calling
David to defend himself in court. Speaking on behalf of the Syrians, the
Ammonites, and the Moabites, Bayle urged:

> Can this method of making war be denied to be blame-
> worthy? Have not the Turks and Tartars a little more
> humanity? And if a vast number of Pamphlets daily
> complain of the military execution of our own time,
> which are really cruel and highly to be blamed, tho mild
> in comparison of David's, what would not the Authors
> of those Pamphlets say at this day, had they such usage
> to censure as the saws, the harrows, and the brick-kilns
> of David, and the general slaughter of all the males, both
> old and young?[14]

Indeed, continues Bayle, "if the people of Syria had been as great Writers
of Libels, as the Europeans are at this day, they would have strangely
disfigured David's glory."[15] In a move anticipatory of deconstruction's

---

13. John Peter Bernard, Thomas Birch, John Lockman et al., *Pierre Bayle. A General
Dictionary, Historical and Critical, in which a New and Accurate Translation of that of the
Celebrated Mr. Bayle, with the Corrections and Observations printed in the late Edition at
Paris, is included* (10 vols.; London, 1734–40), vol. 4, 533; cf. 532–39.

14. Ibid., 536–37. Bayle reads the "saws, the harrows, and the brick-kilns" of 2 Sam.
12:31 as instruments of torture rather than of hard labor.

15. Ibid., 537.

strategic ascription of importance to ostensibly marginal details, he also notes that the Bible unwittingly allows us a glimpse of alternative (perhaps majority?) views of David when it records Shimei's "slander" against the "man of blood" (2 Sam. 16:7).

A later treatise on David, which portrays him as a Nero-like monster of depravity, makes the connection between the historical and the moral question even clearer by describing the obstacles encountered by the reader of the Bible as twofold:

I. The broken unconnected manner in which the Jewish history is transmitted down to us.

II. The partial representation of it, as being written by themselves.[16]

The composite nature of the Old Testament—as an assemblage of *parts*—is here explicitly linked to the question of *partiality*. The Bible's failure to attain to universal moral values, however, is far more catastrophic for this author than its failure to attain to literary unity. For Matthew Tindal, author of *Christianity as Old as the Creation*, it is a failure that must not be glossed over. The Bible's plain sense must not be made palatable through allegory, for instance, however unappetizing that sense may be: "And how can we depend on any Thing said in the Scriptures, if we can't on its Facts? One wou'd think nothing was a plainer Fact, than that of *Lot's* lying with his two Daughers, yet St. Irenaeus allegorises That away. . . ."[17]

In early Enlightenment biblical critique, the fragmented nature of the biblical text is articulated as a subset of the critique of the Bible as all-too-human in the sense of immoral, sinful, and fallen. In a craftily worded mock-lament in his *Characteristics of Men, Manners, Opinions, Times*, Anthony Ashley-Cooper, third Earl of Shaftesbury (1671–1713), plays with the ambiguous boundaries between the superhuman and the subhuman and depicts the Bible as beneath ("beyond") the gentlemanly, the universal, and the humane. Adopting the Calvinist persona of one

---

16. Anon. [John Northoouck], *The History of the Man After God's Own Heart* (Liverpool, 1795; first printed 1761), xi. Implicitly, the immorality of the Bible is ascribed to its foreignness and, specifically, its Jewishness. The tendency in this treatise is to favor "the gospel" (even if that gospel is only loosely connected to the New Testament), and criticize the Old Testament as a foreign, partial, and Jewish book.

17. Matthew Tindal, *Christianity as Old as the Creation: or, The Gospel, a Republication of the Religion of Nature* (London, 1730), 226.

who is too sinful to comprehend the ways of God, but roguishly twisting it, he opines that as a mere philosopher and moralist he is simply too human(e) to appreciate the sacred otherness of the Bible:

> Notwithstanding the pious endeavours which, as devout Christians, we may have used in order to separate ourselves from the interests of mere heathens and infidels, notwithstanding the true pains we may have taken to arm our hearts in behalf of a chosen people against their neighbouring nations of a false religion and worship, there will still be found such a partiality remaining in us towards creatures of the same make and figure as ourselves, as will hinder us from viewing with satisfaction the punishments inflicted by human hands on such aliens and idolaters.
>
> In mere poetry, and the pieces of wit and literature, there is a liberty of thought and an easiness of humour indulged to us in which, perhaps, we are not so well able to contemplate the divine judgements, and see clearly into the justice of those ways which are declared to be so far from our ways and above our highest thoughts or understandings. In such a situation of mind we can hardly endure to see heathen treated as heathen, and the faithful made the executioners of divine wrath. There is a certain perverse humanity in us which inwardly resists the divine commission, though never so plainly revealed. The wit of the best poet is not sufficient to reconcile us to the campaign of a Joshua or the retreat of a Moses by the assistance of an Egyptian loan. Nor will it be possible, by the Muse's art, to make that royal hero appear amiable in human eyes who found such favour in the eye of Heaven. Such are mere human hearts that they can hardly find the least sympathy with that only one which had the character of being after the pattern of the Almighty's.
>
> 'Tis apparent, therefore, that the manners, actions, and characters of sacred writ are in no wise the proper subject of other authors than divines themselves. They are matters incomprehensible in philosophy; they are above the pitch of the mere human historian, the politician, or

the moralist, and are too sacred to be submitted to the poet's fancy when inspirited by no other spirit than that of his profane mistresses the Muses.[18]

This early modern work reveals the deep roots of the notion of the literary as the realm of the human(e), as distinct from the superhuman or the subhuman (the realms of gods or animals)—a notion that still haunts Eagleton's *After Theory* and the contributors to *Theory's Empire*, as we saw. Shaftesbury also risks a relationship between the Bible and literature that is far more radical than most twentieth-century versions of that pairing. Instead of casting the Bible as the perfection of the literary, as recent biblical literary criticism has been prone to do (more on which below), Shaftesbury argues, in an overtly literary piece of writing, that the Bible cannot be translated into the literary since the latter is based on structures of gentlemanliness, empathy, and tolerance, all of which virtues the Bible transgresses and exceeds. Instead of protesting that the Bible is beyond literature, Shaftesbury translates the beyond into the below, and gestures obliquely to the subhuman(e), violent, and intolerant nature of parts of the Bible. As in Kant, these are set up in contrast to the intrinsic morality of the true Bible. The illiberal Bible cannot be translated into the liberal forum of literature (or, indeed, into philosophy, history, politics, or morality) because the "wit of the best poet" cannot make us regard David as a worthy hero, or look on genocide with the requisite sangfroid.

Setting the true spirit against the imperfect letter in order to retrieve a purer moral core, Shaftesbury refers obliquely to what were fast becoming iconic crimes of the Old Testament: the sins of David, the annihilation of the Canaanites, and theft from the Egyptians (these latter two crimes being divinely ordained). To this list many writers added the equally iconic crime of human sacrifice as in the case of Jephthah's daughter, or near-sacrifice as in the case of Isaac. Indeed, the early modern moral critique of the Bible, obsessed as it was with genocide, human sacrifice, and atonement theology, was concerned above all with crimes of blood. In a series of tracts published between 1725 and 1734, Thomas Chubb (1679–1747), one of the lesser-known (read lower-class)

---

18. Anthony, Earl of Shaftesbury, *Characteristics of Men, Manners, Opinions, Times* (ed. John M. Robertson; introduction by Stanley Grean; New York: Bobbs-Merill, 1964 [1711, originally 2 vols.]), Book 1, 229–30.

"Deists,"[19] wrote of Abraham's aborted sacrifice: "No matter if angels, dreams, visions, voices from heaven" affirmed it, "the moral unfitness of the action . . . was a stronger reason against the divinity of the command, than any of those extraordinary ways in which that command was conveyed to him could possibly be for it," for miracles are "directly and immediately evidences only of the power, and not of the veracity or goodness of the agent that performs them."[20] Chubb's response reminds us of the forgotten link between miracles and immoral action as twin branches of the one problem: exceptions to the universal law. Histories of the Enlightenment foreground the battle between miracles and science, forgetting that in a context where science was termed "natural philosophy" and morality "natural law," what we now see as the separate domains of morality and science were conjoined through the complex idea of nature. At a time when the critical fashion was for aspiration to universality, as a putative guarantee of tolerance and peace, anxiety about miracles as a violation of the general laws of nature was matched and exceeded by concern about other exceptional (read violent) acts of the biblical God that likewise violated these laws. Like many of his contemporaries, Chubb grounds "true religion" on the "moral fitness of things," by which he means "an essential difference betwixt good and evil . . . arising from the nature and the relation of things antecedent to, and independent of any divine and human determination concerning them," even, in fact especially, the "arbitrary will and pleasure of God. . . ."[21] By true religion, he means that which is "the same in all ages, in all countries, and in all worlds, (if I may so speak) for if any of the

---

19. As T. L. Bushell argues, Chubb's lowly origins account, in large part, for the curiously minor role accorded to him in twentieth-century treatments of "Deism" (*The Sage of Salisbury: Thomas Chubb, 1679–1747* [New York: Philosophical Library, 1967]). We mark "Deism"/"Deist(s)" in scare quotes as this was a polemical term used to banish certain writers beyond the pale. The writers assembled, mostly by others, under the heading "Deist" do not share a common creed or anti-creed, and rarely found true religion entirely outside the Bible. There are also significant similarities between writers of the period labeled as "orthodox," on the one hand, and "heterodox," on the other, which the label "Deist" masks, a fact insufficiently recognized in classic (and consolidating) treatments of "Deism," such as Henning Graf Reventlow, *The Authority of the Bible and the Rise of the Modern World* (trans. John Bowden; Philadelphia: Fortress Press, 1985).

20. Thomas Chubb, "Treatise XIX: The Case of Abraham with Regard to his offering up Isaac in sacrifice, re-examined, In a Letter to a Clergyman," in idem, *A Collection of Tracts on Various Subjects* (London, 1730), 244.

21. Thomas Chubb, "The Previous Question with regard to Religion," in idem, *A Collection of Tracts*, 211.

other planets are inhabited with creatures constituted, circumstanced, and related as we are, their religion must of course be the same as ours is." Logically, universal religion must extend across the universe and "must govern any life on Mars."[22]

What this means for morally anomalous texts such as the aborted sacrifice of Isaac is made more explicit in Thomas Morgan's *The Moral Philosopher*. Morgan insists that the "Clergy of England" and "systematical divines" must confront the question of whether God's command to Abraham can be "credible" or "probable"—a question they "never care to meddle with; tho' this is the only thing they ought to speak to, if they would say anything to the purpose."[23] Applying intercultural, if not interplanetary, principles of moral fitness and trying to find a response to the conundrum that would satisfy a Martian, or at least the adherents of non-Christian religions, Morgan writes: "It may be probable enough, that either Abraham had such a belief or conceit, or that Moses mistook this case; but that God, in this, or any other case, should dissolve the law of nature and make it a man's duty . . . to act contrary to all the principles and passions or the human constitution, is absolutely incredible."[24] For Morgan as for Chubb, the moral or philosophical question is given priority over the historical question—indeed it exists *antecedently*, or, in Kant's terms, *a priori*. "The thing itself is of such a nature, as *not to be capable of proof by any historical evidence or testimony*," and since "this rational evidence to the understanding" is "*vastly superior and prior to any historical proof*, no such lower proof from testimony can set it aside."[25] In other words, even if an archaeologist were to unearth an indubitably authentic scrap of crumbling parchment signed by God himself, confessing that he had indeed uttered the command of Genesis 22:2 exactly as reported by Moses ("Take now thy son, thine only son Isaac, whom thou lovest, and get thee into the land of Moriah; and offer him there for a burnt offering . . ."), such evidence would have to be

---

22. Ibid., 217.

23. Thomas Morgan, *The Moral Philosopher in a Dialogue between Philalethes, a Christian Deist, and Theophanes, a Christian Jew*; Vol. 3: *Superstition and Tyranny inconsistent with Theocracy Occasioned by the Rev. Dr. Leland's second volume of the Divine Authority of the Old and New Testament Asserted, and the Rev. Mr. Lowman's Dissertation on the Civil Government of the Hebrews* (London, 1740), 134–35.

24. Ibid., 133–34.

25. Thomas Morgan, *The Moral Philosopher in a Dialogue between Philalethes, a Christian Deist, and Theophanes, a Christian Jew*; Vol. 2: *Being a Farther Vindication of Moral Truth and Reason* (London, 1739), 126, emphasis added.

discounted because moral impossibility has been established antecedently or *a priori*. In this mode of reasoning, the question "could it have happened?" is not only one of historical probability but of philosophical and moral possibility, and the latter necessarily takes precedence over the former. What the God of Genesis 22:1-2 reveals to Abraham, then, is precisely the impossibility of that very revelation, and hence of the God thus revealed.[26]

Such ethical accusations were not leveled easily or cleanly against the Bible, however, even by so-called "Deists." The moral critique of the Bible coexisted with the attempted retrieval of a moral core from the Bible. The argument was that one was purging the Bible of accretions (of churchism, priestcraft, foreign ideas, immorality, the mere letter, etc.) in order to retrieve its pure spirit—a spirit that merged with the "gospel" even as that gospel exceeded the mere letter (as it was also already beginning to do for more orthodox thinkers). Universal true religion was tied to Christianity in a way that it was not tied to the religion of the "Tartars," the "Turks," or even the hypothetical Martians. Far from offering a critique of the Bible from a place entirely outside religion, namely, "reason," conceived as religion's other, writers like Bayle represent themselves as caught in a moral dilemma between saving the true God, "eternal Laws," and "true Religion" through the sacrifice of a particular biblical character or text, or sacrificing morality and universal principle in order to save the reputation of a particular person (*un particulier*), such as David.[27] He concludes that the particular must be sacrificed to the general in order to save the "laws of equity" and sustain social stability—for in a culture that takes the Bible seriously as a moral

---

26. Calvin anticipated the eighteenth-century moral critique of the Bible to a degree, albeit from different philosophical and theological premises. Barbara Pitkin writes: "Calvin's low estimate of fallen human nature manifested itself throughout his exegetical work and often distinguished his interpretations from prior and contemporary tradition. For example, in his treatment of the so-called immoralities of the patriarchs, Calvin's criticism were much more severe than those of his predecessors and contemporaries, and he rarely, if ever, drew on any of the traditional excuses offered for patriarchal misbehaviour" ("John Calvin and the Interpretation of the Bible," in *A History of Biblical Interpretation*; Vol. 2: *The Medieval through the Reformation Periods*, ed. Alan J. Hauser and Duane F. Watson [Grand Rapids, Mich.: Eerdmans, 2009], 359). For Calvin, however, the morality of the biblical God was not open to question. Chubb, Morgan, and other eighteenth-century scholars thus take the moral critique of the Bible in an unprecedented direction.

27. Bayle, *A General Dictionary*, Vol. 4, 537–38.

and social exemplar, all kinds of dangerous consequences could follow from favoring *le particulier*.

Even so-called "Deists" like Chubb and Morgan made sure that "true religion" and biblical revelation intersected, or at least touched—albeit in a more complicated ways than they had previously. Whereas they could once have been assumed to be identical, the Bible and natural religion could now unite only through a tangle of convoluted hypotheses. Chubb inaugurated the solution to the Genesis 22 conundrum that would become a staple of subsequent (orthodox) biblical criticism, namely, that God permitted the sacrifice to take place (a subtle adjustment to the claim that he commanded it) in order to teach a moral prohibition against child sacrifice.[28] Morgan for his part, in order to keep natural religion and the sacrifice of Isaac in propinquity, hazarded that the moral corruption might be due to textual corruption: "It may be supposed indeed, that in the short imperfect account of the affair that we have transmitted to us, there may have been some original circumstances relating to it left out, which might have cleared up the whole matter, and rendered the story very reasonable and credible."[29] He went on to hypothesize that such an uncorrupted original would have eliminated misunderstanding by showing how the sacrificial imperative came, not from direct divine command, but from a desire to emulate neighboring Canaanite cultures.

The Eclipse of Biblical Immorality

As these elaborate maneuverings suggest, questions of historical possibility were easier to deal with than questions of moral possibility. Even the "Deists" seemed to recoil from the audacity of charging the biblical God with immorality and declaring Holy Writ antecedently unfit, impossible, or incredible on moral grounds. It is hardly surprising, therefore, that the more orthodox form of emergent biblical criticism entailed taking up the programmatic question "Could it have happened?" in its historical sense while closing the question down in

---

28. Thomas Chubb, "Treatise XVIII: A Supplement to the Previous Question, with regard to Religion. Wherein several objections made to the Previous Question are examined, and in which God's moral character is more fully vindicated. In a Letter to a Friend," in idem, *A Collection of Tracts*, 221–39.

29. Morgan, *The Moral Philosopher*, Vol. 2, 128.

its moral or philosophical sense. In a strategic forgetting, the kind of Enlightenment emblematized by the name of Kant was eclipsed by that emblematized by the name of Darwin. The problem of the miraculous became the paramount problem—a form of deviation from the general laws of nature that stood in for, and displaced, the problem of moral deviation—along with the problem of the text's genesis and evolution. The seemingly tragic tale of faith dashed on the hard rock of fact was actually a relatively happy one for many biblical critics, because by confining the "Could it have happened?" question to the realm of historical or scientific evidence, it gave the biblical God a fighting chance of surviving the impact.

Jonathan Sheehan observes that study of the Bible in the early Enlightenment was conducted under four main headings: historiography, philology, morality, and aesthetics.[30] What he fails to note, however, is that early interrogations of the Bible's morality soon collapsed back into affirmations or assumptions of its morality. Aesthetic approaches to the Bible as literature also evaporated, perhaps for related reasons, because of the distinct mismatch that freethinkers like Shaftesbury perceived between the Bible and the human(e).[31] Moral challenges that were intrinsic to the Enlightenment critique of the Bible in the seventeenth and eighteenth centuries faded back thereafter into the older cultural assumption that the Bible and morality were synonymous. After the eighteenth century, the investigation of biblical morality was quietly dropped from the job description of the biblical scholar. This was because the moral questions put to the Bible by the early rationalists were deemed to be irresolvable and socially corrosive, whereas historical questions were (or so it was imagined) resolvable

---

30. Sheehan structures Part II of his *Enlightenment Bible* around this observation, devoting a chapter to each of the four categories.

31. The first flush of a nascent biblical literary criticism associated with figures such as Robert Lowth and Robert Boyle was followed by what we have come to know as "the eclipse of biblical narrative" (see Hans W. Frei, *The Eclipse of Biblical Narrative: A Study in Eighteenth and Nineteenth Century Hermeneutics* [New Haven, Conn.: Yale University Press, 1974]). More precisely, perhaps, the literary appreciation of the Bible became the province of figures other than the biblical critic—figures such as Matthew Arnold, for instance, who in fact coined the phrase "the Bible as literature," or Richard Green Moulton, author of the highly popular *The Literary Study of the Bible* (Boston: D. C. Heath & Co., 1895) and many other such works. Further on Arnold's and Moulton's Bibles, see David Norton, *A History of the Bible as Literature*; Vol. 2: *From 1700 to the Present Day* (Cambridge: Cambridge University Press, 1993), 368–76.

and less incendiary. Questions of textual corruption, which had coexisted with those of moral corruption, now dominated the emergent field of biblical scholarship, sometimes being used to solve moral problems on the quiet, under another name. The documentary hypothesis, for instance, classically promulgated by Wellhausen in his *Geschichte Israels*,[32] dealt with moral problems covertly. The meticulous separation of the Pentateuch out into four putative sources, designated by the letters J, E, D, and P, can be read retrospectively as an elaborate technical version of the early Enlightenment separation of the Bible's "spirit" from its "letter(s)." Each successive source was seen by Wellhausen and his followers as further away from the moral core, or true spirit, of the biblical religion than its predecessors.[33] As for Morgan, questions of textual corruption or recension mask the attempted recovery of a morally pure text.

Unlike moral errors, textual errors could be rendered useful—in fact infinitely productive. As Sheehan remarks, errors could be used as "evidence for and against genealogical relationships. Not only were they necessary, they were welcome: as evidence of scribal interventions into the text, they made the history of a manuscript legible."[34] Accusations of moral error, in contrast, were insurmountable. They could be studiously avoided, however, by endlessly obsessing over questions of historicity and textual "integrity" (in the sense of literary unity, of course, not of moral soundness). They could further be avoided by retreat to what Kant would have seen as the pre-modern or pre-critical position: an assumption of the synonymy of Bible and morality, or a resumption, at least, of the old task of surreptitiously making the Bible more moral. Thus the category of the historical in biblical scholarship became a surrogate not only for the ethical but also for the theological, and did not disturb either category directly. Challenges to the Bible's historicity and morality were significant primarily because they called its theological

---

32. Julius Wellhausen, *Geschichte Israels* (Berlin, 1878). Every subsequent edition of the work was entitled *Prolegomena zur Geschichte Israels*, from whence it made its way into English as *Prolegomena to the History of Israel*.

33. A (Reformed) tale that even the book's table of contents tells; for example, "II.1 In the earliest period of the history of Israel there is no distinction between clergy and laity. . . . III.1 In the oldest part of JE there are no priests. . . ." Julius Wellhausen, *Prolegomena to the History of Israel* (trans. J. Sutherland Black and Allan Menzies; Edinburgh: A. & C. Black, 1885), xiii.

34. Sheehan, *The Enlightenment Bible*, 105.

authority into question. But the challenge to theological authority could be blunted by sidelining both the theological and the ethical in favor of the historical. Theological authority came to be treated obliquely through the proxy domain of history. As a result, debates over historicity became convoluted, fraught, and obsessive in biblical studies—and remain so to this day.

The historical now served as a place marker for the theological, but also, paradoxically, as a license to do biblical scholarship in a thoroughly de-theologized mode, one that shattered every biblical-scholarly mold that had been handed down since antiquity. Hence the epistemic rupture that we discussed earlier. Yet it was not as though the biblical scholar could no longer hold theological beliefs. On the contrary, the removal of the theological as the target of critical inquiry ensured that he could be both a skeptic and a believer at one and the same time. It became possible to be at once Christian and "modern," theologically orthodox yet simultaneously skeptical of the Bible's historicity—though a complex series of markers were set in place to regulate how far one might push one's skepticism. The boundaries shifted across national borders (for example, "radical" Germans vs. "moderate" Britons) and from one period to the next, scholars gravely hopping one-legged up to the line and back again on such issues as the existence of the historical Moses or the factuality of Jesus' resurrection. Knotty and thorny as it was, the question of the miracle as the implausible exception to natural law was far easier to swallow than the question of morally exceptional divine behavior in deviation from moral principle. Questioning the Bible's supernaturalism increasingly became a non-controversial practice, while questioning the Bible's morality became a cultural marker of heterodoxy.

Critical study of the Bible in its formative period, then, was established in a paradoxical cultural space, altogether unrestricted and severely circumscribed at one and the same time. Such study could stretch vertiginously into a daunting number of disciplinary domains—ancient history, philology, archaeology, long-dead languages of the ancient Near East, Greco-Roman literature and philosophy, ancient geography, numismatics, botany, and more—and quests for all manner of elusive scholarly grails: for the biblical autographs, reduced by time to a myriad of fragmentary and contradictory copies; for the putative sources underlying those original texts; for the authors who wrote the texts and the communities for which they wrote them; for the authorial intentions needed to unify the texts and infuse them with coherent meaning; and for all the other assorted intangibles calculated ever to hover, carrot-like, beyond the critic's reach and so draw the grand enterprise of biblical scholarship inexorably onward and upward.

The domain of the biblical scholar increasingly became that of the Letter, distinct to a not insignificant degree from the Spirit, in the sense of that which is essential to salvation. It was not that the Bible did not intersect to a considerable degree with theology, morality, religion, and, indeed, the Spirit, but it was also perceived as containing letters in surplus; or, as Lessing cannily put it, the relationship between the Spirit/morality/religion and the Bible was akin to that between net and gross.[35] With the notion that the Bible exceeds religion in the sense that it contains in abundance material that is less or other than religion, the Bible entered into a second life as document or text. It became possible to do almost anything with this Bible-as-text—provided that anything took the preapproved form of historical-critical analysis and hypothesis. For there is no end of things that one can do with the letter, especially the letter of the Bible, forever severed from its human senders and intended receivers, and so always purloined by the scholar en route to a destination at which it can now never fully arrive (not that it actually ever could).[36]

It was not, however, the case that theological truth was thereby banished from biblical scholarship altogether; rather, it was exiled to the margins or relegated to a postscript. But the repressed tended to return, as the repressed tends to do. Typically, for instance, theological truth might be reaffirmed in a closing paragraph, or an appendix to the work proper, and hence to the proper work of the biblical scholar. The work might end in a coda of faith, a confessional idiom that jarred with the scientism of the main study.

Several consequences flowed from the inability of biblical scholarship to digest the theological, to pass it through the critical system. First, it led to awkwardness, even antipathy, between the disciplines of theology and biblical studies, disciplines that are still uncomfortable around

---

35. G. E. Lessing, *Cambridge Free Thoughts and Letters on Bibliolatry* (ed. Isaac Bernard; trans. H. H. Bernard; London: Trübner & Co., 1862), 23, near the beginning of a section entitled "The Bible manifestly contains more than belongs to Religion."

36. Cf. Jacques Derrida, *The Post Card: From Socrates to Freud and Beyond* (trans. Alan Bass; Chicago: University of Chicago Press, 1987), 489.

each other, like one-time lovers who no longer know quite what to say or how to behave in each other's company. Second, it predestined to failure the subdiscipline of "biblical theology," an enterprise that, despite repeated attempts to rise out of its own ashes, has appeared singularly unsuccessful to the majority of biblical scholars, not in the sense that such attempts have been incompetently executed but in the sense that the coupling of a certain style of theology—systematic or even proto-systematic—with the term "biblical" has seemed to constitute a category mistake. Third, theology *has* flourished in some sectors of biblical studies, particularly, and not accidentally, in New Testament studies. Most notably, for the past half-century or so, Gospel scholars have been centrally concerned with the individual theologies of the Evangelists, and for considerably longer than that, Pauline scholars have been preoccupied with the theology of Paul. The way in which such theological inquiry is typically conducted, however, confirms rather than disconfirms our argument. The Fourth Gospel, for instance, could be pulverized to rubble, and regularly has been, on the level of historicity.[37] But if the typical Johannine scholar has wielded a hammer in one hand with which to attack the historical issues thrown up by the Gospel, he or she has held a feather duster in the other hand with which to treat its theology. The same has been true for the scholarly treatment of the Pauline letters, except that here the hammer has often been abandoned altogether. What David Clines asserts of biblical scholars in general is most of all true of Pauline scholars: "Not one academic biblical scholar in a hundred will tell you that their primary task is to *critique* the Bible. For some reason, we have convinced ourselves that our business is simply to *understand*, to *interpret*."[38] For the overwhelming majority of New Testament scholars, and not just of the Pauline stripe, it has sufficed to gloss, paraphrase, amplify, annotate, or otherwise elaborate on the theology, Christology, pneumatology, ecclesiology, and eschatology of the New Testament authors. The story the given Gospel told could be

---

37. "The entire historical-Jesus enterprise, as it exists today, is inherently set against the Fourth Gospel and every other potential source that does not fit the Synoptic mold." Tom Thatcher, "Introduction: The John, Jesus, and History Project," in *John, Jesus, and History*; Vol. 1: *Critical Appraisals of Critical Views*, ed. Paul N. Anderson, Felix Just, S.J., and Tom Thatcher (Society of Biblical Literature Symposium Series, 44; Leiden: Brill, 2007), 10–11.

38. David J. A. Clines, *The Bible and the Modern World* (The Biblical Seminar, 51: Sheffield: Sheffield Academic, 1997), 23, his emphasis.

shown, implicitly or even explicitly, to be largely fictional; the theology for which that story was the vehicle could not. Liberal Protestantism could live with a dedivinized Jesus set loose in a dehistoricized gospel, but it could not live with an equally reduced God. In particular it could not live with an immoral God, nor even with an immoral Jesus.

The First and Third Quests for the Moral Jesus

The nineteenth-century marriage of the Enlightenment Bible and the Moral Bible is exemplified by the liberal quest for the historical Jesus. Whereas a century earlier the issue had been the apparent immorality of the biblical deity, the issue now was the paradigmatic morality of the authentic teaching of the historical Jesus as salvaged and reconstructed by the critical scholar. The exemplary moral teaching ascribed to the historical Jesus becomes, in effect, the canon within the canon, the yardstick (*kanon* in Greek) against which all other ethical systems, whether inside or outside the Bible, must be measured—and, of course, found wanting, not least the ethical systems of ancient Israel and those of Judaism of any era. Because this intracanonical canon is a moral canon, morality is the living heart that beats within the corpus of Scripture, beneath its paper-thin flesh, a heart accessible to the delicately honed critical instruments of the historical Jesus quester. For earlier thinkers such as Kant, Bayle, Shaftesbury, Chubb, and Morgan, as we saw, the God of universal moral perfection coincided only imperfectly with the imperfect biblical God, and the immorality of certain biblical texts and characters became an overt problem. But now the ultimate standard for morality was once again securely located within the Bible itself (though it readily appears in retrospect to have been the patriarchal, anti-Judaic, and imperialistic morality of nineteenth-century liberal Protestantism). Furthermore, even if Jesus of Nazareth was no longer to be regarded as supernaturally divine, he could at least be regarded as the supreme agent or instrument of the divine, so that his unique moral system could be seen to stem ultimately from God. It was divine even if he was not. Thus it comes about that not only is ultimate morality reinstated in the heart of the Bible, as in the pre-critical era in biblical scholarship, but an absolutely moral God is reinstated along with it. And thereby the wound opened up by the early modern incision—the assault on the morality of the biblical God—is surreptitiously sutured, perhaps even without the cognizance of the historical Jesus questers themselves. Busily their fingers fly over the stitches while their minds are occupied elsewhere.

This is not to say, however, that the First Quest for the historical Jesus was innocent of more severe surgical instruments—the lancet, the bone saw, the surgical scissors. The dissective proclivities of the First Quest found concrete, emblematic expression in the methodology of its most famous son, Thomas Jefferson, who literally cut the New Testament Gospels to shreds with a scissors. Jefferson meticulously cut verse after verse out of the Gospel texts of his King James version.[39] He then sutured the amputated verses together and mounted them on the pages of a blank book. The result was a forty-six-page octavo, which he subsequently enlarged to eighty-two pages, titling it *The Life and Morals of Jesus of Nazareth*.[40] And the purpose of this Frankensteinian experiment? As Jefferson explained it to fellow statesman John Adams in a letter of 1813:

> In extracting the pure principles which he [Jesus] taught, we should have to strip off the artificial vestments in which they have been muffled by priests, who have travestied them into various forms, as instruments of riches and power to themselves. . . . We must reduce our volume to the simple evangelists, select, even from them, the very words only of Jesus, paring off the amphibologisms into which they have been led, by forgetting often, or not understanding, what had fallen from him, by giving their own misconceptions as his dicta, and expressing unintelligibly for others what they had not understood themselves. *There will be found remaining the most sublime*

---

39. As did the committee that produced *The Woman's Bible*, interestingly, though for rather different reasons: "Each person purchased two Bibles, ran through them from Genesis to Revelation, marking all the texts that concerned women. The passages were cut out, and pasted in a blank book, and the commentaries then written underneath" (Elizabeth Cady Stanton, "Preface," in idem et al., *The Woman's Bible*, 6).

40. The work was published posthumously in 1904 by order of the United States congress as *The Life and Morals of Jesus of Nazareth: Extracted Textually from the Gospels in Greek, Latin, French, and English* (Washington, D.C.: Government Printing Office, 1904). Further on Jefferson's dissective hermeneutic, see Stephen D. Moore, *God's Gym: Divine Male Bodies of the Bible* (London and New York: Routledge, 1996), 42–43.

*and benevolent code of morals which has ever been offered
to man.* I have performed this operation for my own use,
by cutting verse by verse out of the printed book, and
arranging the matter which is evidently his, and which
is as easily distinguishable as diamonds in a dunghill.[41]

This fervent moral vision is, however, also a sinister (and immoral) one;
for the dunghill, for Jefferson, is essentially Jewish.[42] A little earlier in
the same letter to Adams, Jefferson quotes approvingly and at length
from a contemporary anti-Jewish rant on the "the low state of moral
philosophy" in rabbinic Judaism occasioned by the "wretched depravity
of sentiment and manners" that characterizes it. "It was the reformation
of this 'wretched depravity' of morals which Jesus undertook," adds
Jefferson[43]—and then proceeds with the encomium to Jesus' incomparable
moral code quoted above. To be worthy of what Kant would have
termed "moral faith," Jesus must first be separated from his Jewishness.

Yet if the First Quest soared on a vision of an unprecedented, unpar-
alleled, and universal morality located at the centre of Christian scripture, it also foundered on that vision. The First Quest is commonly said
to have been brought to an end by the appearance in 1906 of Albert
Schweitzer's *Von Reimarus zu Wrede*.[44] Schweitzer's argument is ordinarily framed as a historical one: basing himself uncompromisingly on
material in the Synoptic Gospels that imputes an imminent eschatology
to Jesus (e.g., Mark 9:1; 13:30; Matt. 10:23), Schweitzer argued, against
earlier First Questers,[45] that the historical Jesus was an apocalyptic

---

41. Letter to John Adams, October 13, 1813, in *The Writings of Thomas Jefferson*,
ed. Andrew A. Lipscomb and Albert Ellery Bergh (Washington, D.C.: Thomas Jefferson
Memorial Association of the United States, 1903–1904), vol. 13, 389–90, emphasis added.
We are grateful to Thomas Fabisiak for drawing our attention to this letter.

42. Anti-Judaism is, indeed, indissociable from the First Quest. The writings of its
putative progenitor, H. R. Reimarus, for example, are laced with anti-Judaic polemic,
while Ernest Renan, another of the First Quest's most prominent scholars, is commonly
regarded as one of the architects of anti-Semitism as a modern racial ideology.

43. Jefferson, Letter to John Adams, 389.

44. Albert Schweitzer, *Von Reimarus zu Wrede: Eine Geschichte der Leben-Jesu-
Forschung* (Tübingen: J. C. B. Mohr [Paul Siebeck], 1906). An expanded second edition
appeared in 1913 under the title *Geschichte der Leben-Jesu-Forschung*. The quotations
below are from the English translation of the second edition: *The Quest of the Historical
Jesus* (trans. William Montgomery, J. R. Coates, Susan Cupitt, and John Bowden; Minneapolis: Fortress Press, 2001).

45. But in continuity with the work of Johannes Weiss, as is also commonly noted.

prophet. At a more fundamental level, however, Schweitzer's argument was a moral one. What he did was to pull the moral rug from under the First Questers' Jesus of Nazareth, arguing the latter's exorbitant ethic, epitomized by the Sermon on the Mount, to be merely an "interim ethic" formulated to fill the fraught but compressed time period leading up to his imagined apocalyptic return. "To attempt to work out a complete ethical system for ourselves from Jesus' ethic is senseless and absurd," Schweitzer concluded.[46]

Implicitly, the nails that Schweitzer drove into the coffin of the First Quest's Jesus were Kantian ones: "Our modern social ethic, like our metaphysic and world-view, must evolve rationally and takes its shape in accordance with natural and inherent principles. Jesus can no more become the foundation to our ethic than he can be the foundation to our religion. He can only provide an element in it, albeit a powerfully determinate one."[47] What is not generally recognized is the extent to which Schweitzer's immensely influential verdict on the apocalyptic Jesus whom he (re)constructed entailed a smooth recycling of what we earlier termed the "first wave" of Enlightenment challenge to the Bible, a challenge emblematized by the name of Kant. For Schweitzer as for Kant, the moral question was paramount, the historical question merely a subset of it. The fundamental problem for Schweitzer was not that the eschatological worldview of his Jesus of Nazareth could not be reconciled with the worldview of the post-Enlightenment historian; the fundamental problem was rather that the eschatology relativized the Nazarene's moral teaching, localized it to an ancient historical and cultural context, and thereby turned it into an intractable philosophical problem for the modern Christian.

Much of the seminal work produced under the aegis of the contemporary "Third Quest" for the historical Jesus, winding down as we write, may be read as an implicit attempt to do an end run around the barrier erected by Schweitzer and make Jesus of Nazareth an unambiguously fitting subject once more for a "moral faith" in the Kantian

---

46. Schweitzer, *The Quest of the Historical Jesus*, 455.

47. Ibid. Schweitzer was both deeply critical of Kant and irresistibly drawn to him, choosing to write his doctoral thesis on Kant's philosophy of religion. See further James Brabazon, *Albert Schweitzer: A Biography* (2nd ed.; New York: Syracuse University Press, 2000), 69–75. Brabazon argues that the "emphasis on a basic principle of ethics impressed Schweitzer more than anything else about Kant" (ibid., 72).

mold. Much of the Third Quest for the *historical* Jesus has, in other words, been a Third Quest for the *moral* Jesus. Once again, as so often since the nineteenth century, the theological and moral authority of the Bible is being treated obliquely, by proxy, and in blinkered fashion through obsessive investigation of the Bible's historicity. The critical methods employed by the Third Questers are more sophisticated than those employed by the First Questers, and the anti-Judaism and anti-Semitism that dogged the First Quest are now thoroughly renounced in principle. But the ethics ascribed to the historical Jesus by many of the Third Questers are regularly accompanied by claims reminiscent in their absoluteness of the nineteenth-century claims. Tellingly, the most extravagant claims for the revolutionary and exemplary—and, not infrequently, divine—character of the Galilean peasant's ethics have stemmed from the Jesus Seminar, ostensibly the most critical and skeptical wing of historical Jesus research.[48] The way in which the Seminar famously stripped and flayed the biblical text, irreverently cutting and hacking to get at its authentic core, yet always reverently holding up that heart, once it had been cut out, as a core of teaching that was exemplarily ethical,[49] perfectly illustrated the conflicted way in which biblical scholarship has tended to operate since the nineteenth century. It has slashed away at the biblical text with one hand, pitilessly lopping

---

48. See, for example, the work of John Dominic Crossan, especially *The Historical Jesus: The Life of a Mediterranean Jewish Peasant* (San Francisco: HarperSanFrancisco, 1991) and *Jesus: A Revolutionary Biography* (San Francisco: HarperSanFrancisco, 1994), and that of Marcus Borg, especially *Jesus: A New Vision* (San Francisco: Harper & Row, 1987), *Meeting Jesus Again for the First Time: The Historical Jesus and the Heart of Contemporary Faith* (San Francisco: HarperSanFrancisco, 1995), and *Jesus: Uncovering the Life, Teachings, and Relevance of a Religious Revolutionary* (San Francisco: HarperSanFrancisco, 2006).

49. Crossan implicitly sutures the gash that Schweitzer had opened up between the historical Jesus' ethic and an acceptable contemporary ethic, the latter, for Crossan, being an egalitarian ethic profoundly subversive of any hierarchical status quo: "What he [Jesus] was saying and doing was as unacceptable in the first as in the twentieth century, there, here, or anywhere" (Crossan, *The Historical Jesus*, xii). It has been left to other Third Questers to play the Schweitzerian spoiler role in relation to the attractively contemporary Jesus of Crossan, Borg, and other Jesus Seminarians through counter-construction of an apocalyptic Jesus altogether more alien to the Western liberal mindset. See especially Dale C. Allison, *Jesus of Nazareth: Millenarian Prophet* (Minneapolis: Fortress Press, 1998); Bart D. Ehrman, *Jesus: Apocalyptic Prophet of the New Millenium* (Oxford: Oxford University Press, 1999); and Paula Fredriksen, *Jesus of Nazareth, King of the Jews: A Jewish Life and the Emergence of Christianity* (New York: Alfred A. Knopf, 1999).

off all that it deemed unhistorical or secondary with its finely honed critical scalpel, while reflexively holding the text's ethics and theology in a protective grasp with the other hand. So deeply ingrained is the habit, moreover, that the operation has ordinarily proceeded as an unconscious act, the right hand not knowing what the left is doing.[50]

This curious way of doing biblical criticism, however, has not entirely held sway, and certainly not since the field has ceased being populated almost entirely by ordained churchmen. The eighteenth-century assault on the morality of the biblical text, and even the morality of the biblical God, is now being replayed in a different register. The critique might not be entirely new, but it has achieved unprecedented momentum. Anticipated by periodic female voices in the wilderness, most notably that of Elizabeth Cady Stanton, principal author of the late Victorian *The Woman's Bible*,[51] feminist biblical critics in the 1970s and 1980s effectively reopened the interrogation of biblical morality begun by figures like Kant, Bayle, and Shaftesbury—and also pushed it into areas of which those venerable gentlemen could not have dreamed, except in nightmare. Ethical interrogation of biblical texts has also been integral to that diffuse enterprise known as "ideological criticism,"[52] as well as to certain expressions of postcolonial biblical criticism.[53] In each of these recent challenges to biblical morality, the early modern strategy of holding the Bible accountable to an ethical standard that is in some sense beyond or outside the Bible has resurfaced after centuries of hiatus. Ethical criticism is once again an active element of biblical scholarship; and so while biblical scholarship has seemingly drifted far from its early Enlightenment moorings, in another sense it has simply returned to port.

---

50. For a set of attempts to think the historical Jesus outside the usual historicist and ecclesiastical boxes, see Halvor Moxnes, Ward Blanton, and James G. Crossley, eds., *Jesus beyond Nationalism: Constructing the Historical Jesus in a Period of Cultural Complexity* (BibleWorld; London: Equinox, 2010).

51. See n. 2 above.

52. On which see The Bible and Culture Collective, *The Postmodern Bible* (New Haven, Conn.: Yale University Press, 1995), 272–308.

53. Such as Tat-siong Benny Liew, *Politics of Parousia: Reading Mark Inter(con)textually* (Biblical Interpretation Series, 42; Leiden: Brill, 1999), Musa W. Dube, *Postcolonial Feminist Interpretation of the Bible* (St. Louis: Chalice, 2000), or Joseph A. Marchal, *The Politics of Heaven: Women, Gender, and Empire in the Study of Paul* (Paul in Critical Contexts; Minneapolis: Fortress Press, 2008).

The Moral Minority

At this point a familiar move suggests itself.[54] We should surely show, as we have indeed shown in previous work,[55] how the old, ironically obfuscated Enlightenment extolled a very different morality than the kind found in feminist and other gender criticisms, ideological criticism, postcolonial criticism, and "reading[s] from this place."[56] Prejudices are painfully close to the surface in the older moral critiques, as we have already seen. There are no prizes for spotting that the eighteenth-century treatise that connects the "broken unconnected" nature of the Old Testament texts to "Jewish partiality"[57] is not only linking nascent "historical criticism" to moral critique but linking moral critique in turn to the expulsion of the Jew(ish) as the inner-biblical alien. New modes of biblical scholarship reenergized old Christian habits of supersessionism. Anti-Judaism became a stock feature of much modern biblical criticism because the figure of the "virtual Jew" was fundamental to the putative extraction of a proto-Christian moral core from the Old Testament and the often insufficiently new New Testament. In consequence, as we saw, such prominent products of Enlightenment biblical scholarship as the First Quest for the historical Jesus were anti-Jewish in ways that were more than superficial. The ancient sparks between the New and

---

54. This section began as a response to Hans Leander, "The Returning Jesus as a Moral Problem," an unpublished paper presented at the Society of Biblical Literature Annual Meeting in New Orleans, November 2009. Having read an early draft of the present chapter, Leander urged us to draw more of a distinction between Enlightenment and contemporary forms of moral critique.

55. See, for example, Moore, *God's Gym*; Yvonne M. Sherwood, *The Prostitute and the Prophet: Hosea's Marriage in Literary-Theoretical Perspective* (Journal for the Study of the Old Testament Supplement Series, 212; Sheffield: Sheffield Academic, 1996; reprinted as *The Prostitute and the Prophet: Reading Hosea in the Late Twentieth Century* [London: T. & T. Clark, 2004]); idem, "Jonah the Jew: The Evolution of a Biblical Character," in idem, *A Biblical Text and Its Afterlives: The Survival of Jonah in Western Culture* (Cambridge: Cambridge University Press, 2000), 21–31; and idem, "'Colonising the Old Testament' or 'Representing Christian Interests Abroad': Jewish-Christian Relations across Old Testament Territory," in *Christian-Jewish Relations through the Centuries*, ed. Stanley E. Porter and Brook W. R. Pearson (Journal for the Study of the Old Testament Supplement Series 192; Sheffield: Sheffield Academic, 2000), 255–81.

56. For the eponymous example of this genre, see Fernando F. Segovia and Mary Ann Tolbert eds., *Reading from This Place*; Vol. 1: *Social Location and Biblical Interpretation in the United States*; Vol. 2: *Social Location and Biblical Interpretation in Global Perspective* (Minneapolis: Fortress Press, 1995).

57. See p. 52 above.

the Old, Christian and Jew, ignited the modern engine of critique. Some of the Enlightenment texts we considered earlier also seem to beg the now standard exposé of the hubris inherent in the universals they extol. What better example of the totalizing pretensions of the European-universal than the belief that the principles of religion, law, reason, and humanity that define Europe must extend not just across the entire globe but even to other planets? The postulation of such international—and interplanetary—universals implicitly legitimate Europe's practical governance of all other races—even Martians.[58]

Continued exposé of the moral myopia of the past remains crucial, not least in the task of writing genealogies of biblical criticism that no longer locate the field in some implausible, depoliticized vacuum of neutrality where change is driven purely by the advancement of knowledge. But the strategy of exposé is also dangerous on two counts. It serves to locate us, a little too snugly and a little too smugly, as architects of a greater, truer Enlightenment—one finally prepared to dismantle the "universal" truth of the less enlightened Enlightenment in defence of the local truths of the female, the minority, the subaltern. It also serves to set the truth of the One or universal in dichotomous contrast to the truths of the local or particular, with right clearly on one side and not the other. The totalizing One of early modern certainty, epitomised by the moral myopia of an elite white gentlemen's club, is thereby juxtaposed with a "postmodern" collapse of faith in universals.

There may, however, be other ways of talking about this contrast—ways that are more unsettling, more interesting, and more risky. There may be other ways of reading the difference between a form of moral critique whose energy derives from the postulation of universals so transcendental in ambition as to press beyond the international toward the interplanetary, and another form of moral critique whose energy derives from statements of identity bound up with race/place, gender/ sex, and other such territorial and bodily loci. Whereas Shaftesbury could protest against the ungentlemanly conduct of Joshua as a transgression against all human/moral values, a contemporary moral critic such as Robert Allen Warrior will protest against the genocide of the Canaanites from the perspective of an Osage Indian, or a host of feminist critics will protest against the abuse of actual or symbolic women

---

58. See pp. 54–56 above.

in the Prophets or the Apocalypse.[59] What does it mean that this resurgent moral critique of the Bible is conducted in the name of somatically marked and culturally valorized subject positions? Are there ways of questioning the current close connection between identity and moral critique without subscribing to reactionary attempts to protect an imagined pure humanity, pure literature, or pure scripture?

The difference between the two modes of moral critique—those of the Enlightenment and contemporary identity politics—can be suggestively reframed using Wendy Brown's astute history of "tolerance" in her *Regulating Aversion: Tolerance in the Age of Identity and Empire*.[60] Brown reads the difference between the seventeenth and eighteenth centuries, on the one hand, and the contemporary, on the other, in ways that challenge the latter, rather than celebrate our relative freedom from former myopias. She tracks how tolerance in the early modern sense was birthed in the Lockeian campaign for (limited) freedom of religion, and was predicated on the premise that "man" was a universal creature, only contingently divided by language, culture, nation, or ethnicity and therefore free to choose his sites of belief and unbelief. Late twentieth- and early twenty-first-century tolerance, in contrast, flourishes on the premise of intractable contrast and difference. In a relatively recent *volte-face*, tolerance has settled around the "ascriptive identity" of a person.[61] There has been a major shift "from a universal subject imagined to arrive at particular beliefs or values through revelation or deliberation" to "a particular subject (of sexuality, ethnicity, etc.) who is thought to have these beliefs or values by virtue of who he or she is."[62] These late modern days, "marked identities ranging from black to lesbian to Jew" are understood "to issue from a core truth that generates certain

---

59. Robert Allen Warrior, "Canaanites, Cowboys and Indians: Deliverance, Conquest and Liberation Theology Today," in *The Postmodern Bible Reader*, ed. David Jobling, Tina Pippin, and Ronald Schleifer (Oxford: Blackwell, 2001), 188–94. See also, for example, Renita Weems, *Battered Love: Marriage, Sex, and Violence in the Hebrew Prophets* (Minneapolis: Fortress Press, 1995); Sherwood, *The Prostitute and the Prophet*; and Tina Pippin, "The Heroine and the Whore: The Apocalypse of John in Feminist Perspective," in *From Every People and Nation: The Book of Revelation in Intercultural Perspective*, ed. David Rhoads (Minneapolis: Fortress Press, 2005), 127–46.

60. Wendy Brown, *Regulating Aversion: Tolerance in the Age of Identity and Empire* (Princeton, N.J.: Princeton University Press, 2005).

61. Ibid., 47.

62. Ibid., 46.

beliefs, practises and experiences in the world."[63] According to Brown, this most recent version of tolerance is "predicated on a peculiarly modern discourse of the subject" in which "opinions, belief, and practises are cast not as matters of conscience, education, or revelation but as the material of the person of which certain attributes (racial, sexual, gendered, or ethnic) are an index: hence the notion of 'black consciousness' or 'queer sensibility.'"[64]

Of course, in postcolonial and gender theory, racial and sexual identities are characteristically construed as hybrid, fluid, and non-essentialist.[65] Nevertheless, in public policy and even in academia in the West, we cannot seem to get past a certain obstinate essentialism that lingers around the brute fact of being "black" or "Asian" or "gay" or "transgendered" in a way that it does not around, say, being "working class."[66] Identity now finds its most secure anchors in sex and race, and relatedly in nationalisms and subnationalisms. As Foucault famously argued, the homosexual has been produced in modernity as a "type of life, a life form," such that "nothing that [goes] into his total composition [is] unaffected by his sexuality."[67] Class, perceived as extrinsic, contingent, and mobile, is the weakest element in the threefold mantra of "sex, race, and class."

Academic moral critique organized around identity runs the risk of overbuilding local sites of truth while undergirding the widespread loss of common epistemological authority for the political and ethical.[68] The academy becomes a mirror of society and the political, understood as "places where individuals with fixed identities, interests, and ideas chafe and bargain" as they work toward the modest goal of "civic cohabitation."[69] As the "beacon of multicultural justice and civic peace at the

---

63. Ibid., 42.

64. Ibid., 43.

65. See the now classic formulations in, for example, Homi K. Bhabha, *The Location of Culture* (London and New York: Routledge, 1994); Judith Butler, *Gender Trouble: Feminism and the Subversion of Identity* (London and New York: Routledge, 1990); and Eve Kosofsky Sedgwick, *Epistemology of the Closet* (Berkeley and Los Angeles: University of California Press, 1990).

66. Cf. Brown, *Regulating Aversion*, 47.

67. Michael Foucault, *The History of Sexuality*; Vol. 1: *An Introduction* (trans. Robert Hurley; New York: Random House, 1978), 43.

68. Cf. Brown, *Regulating Aversion*, 39.

69. Ibid., 89, 11.

turn of the twenty-first century,"[70] tolerance insists that readings from different places be given a place, even as that place is by definition partial (in both senses of the term) and local—and all the more valorized for being so. If a minority is marked *as* a minority only when it poses a challenge to the majority, the politics of tolerance and the *telos* of multicultural citizenship systematically defuse that challenge by calling on all identities, whether minor or major, to nonconfrontational coexistence.

Contemporary moral critique of the Bible is largely conducted in the name of certain marked identities or signs of acceptable difference. "Critique," from the Greek term *kritikē*, carries multiple related senses, among them "separating," "judging," "fighting," and "accusing." More often than not in our present disciplinary moment, the always risky practice of a biblical studies professional separating himself or herself from the biblical text on ideological or moral grounds—"judging" it, "fighting" it, "accusing" it—is associated with declaration of a minority identity. Such sites of identity are widely recognized and tolerated sites of separation from the majority, and as such also serve to explain and legitimate separation between the particular scholar and the biblical text. It is acceptable to critique the Bible as an African American, for example, or as a lesbian of any race or ethnicity, because the attack is being carried out in the name of subject positions and sites of difference that are widely acknowledged as demanding respect, and nowhere more than in the academy. Such critique is often made in the name of pain, victimization, and injustice. We hear and must hear the voices of those who have been damaged by a Bible that has repeatedly lent itself to racist, sexist, homophobic, colonizing, and other dehumanizing agendas. Such battles stage a clash of identities that, under the aegis of tolerance, demand a hearing in the public and academic spheres.[71]

The question nonetheless arises: might moral critique of the Bible today take other legitimate forms? What would it mean—would it even be possible—to voice moral critique of the Bible in the name of

---

70. Ibid., 1, 3.

71. For discussion of a recent case where respect for the Bible collides with respect for gay rights, and a further discussion of the paradoxes of rights, respect, and identity politics, see Yvonne Sherwood, "The Bible in a Glass Case: Reflections on a Recent Case of Blasphemy, 'Defacing,' and Saving the Bible's Public Face," in idem, *Biblical Blaspheming: Trials of the Sacred for a Secular Age* (Cambridge: Cambridge University Press, forthcoming).

something infinitesimally small (and unprotected) like a single I, or, conversely, in the name of a general ethic? In the name even of a "universal"? We return to these complex questions in the next chapter.[72]

The Problems of the Biblical Scholar

What biblical scholarship became during its formative period was a far cry from what literary scholarship would become. Ironically, however, it was biblical scholarship that originally provided literary scholarship with the model for close reading of the literary text. Morris Dickstein notes that prior to the twentieth century, detailed analyses of individual works of literature are almost nonexistent, while before the nineteenth century "even essays devoted to individual authors are a rarity."[73] With few exceptions, nascent literary scholarship had no model, framework, or rationale for line-by-line interpretation or even contextual analysis. The exceptions included the Neoplatonic commentaries on Plato, medieval analyses of Aristotle, and Samuel Johnson's *Lives of the Poets*. Far and away the most notable exception, however, was the tradition of biblical commentary, which would provide the model for both literary scholarship (textual criticism, annotated editions, and the like) and literary criticism (explication of the meaning of words, lines, passages, and entire works).[74] But the influence did not flow only in one direction. As the "higher criticism" of the Bible developed, "it repaid this secular scholarship the compliment of imitation," as Dickstein puts it.[75]

It would be a mistake, however, to imagine that, as a result of this mutual mimicry, a situation eventually developed in which there was

---

72. See pp. 116–22 below. A lesser question trails these larger questions. Might it even be possible, as apparently it was for the eighteenth-century "Deists," to deal humorously, even playfully, with the Bible in the process of voicing moral critique of its horrors and absurdities? Contemporary moral critique of the Bible mirrors the seriousness and passion of eighteenth-century scholarship while seldom undertaking the risk of levity and irreverence also characteristic of it. Are we late modern biblical scholars compelled to be more sober in our scholarship than our early modern counterparts? What unwritten rules insist that we be more solemn and formal in our relations to the Bible while declaring our disagreements with it, even though (in fact probably because) we no longer participate in Shaftesbury's gentlemanly communion of politesse?

73. Morris Dickstein, "The Rise and Fall of 'Practical' Criticism: From I. A. Richards to Barthes and Derrida," in *Theory's Empire: An Anthology of Dissent*, ed. Daphne Patai and Will H. Corral (New York: Columbia University Press, 2005), 65.

74. Ibid.

75. Ibid.

not much to distinguish biblical and literary scholarship in terms of characteristic disciplinary preoccupations. Significant differences were there from the start, and intensified with the passage of time. By the early 1960s, René Wellek had already lived long enough to be able to amuse his comparative literature class at Yale by recalling a seminar on Goethe's *Faust* that he himself had taken as a student that began with sources so distantly antecedent to *Faust* that the seminar never quite succeeded in arriving at *Faust*.[76] Of course, it would require no tenuous oral tradition strung out over the generations to provide matching anec-dotes from biblical scholarship. Much of our discipline would still read-ily recognize many of its most passionate investments in most of what the New Critics resolutely set aside in the 1930s and 1940s, beginning with the "background" of the literary text, including its relationship to antecedent texts. "Sources and analogues—*Quellenforschung*, philology, along with social and biographical contexts—belonged to the old histor-ical scholarship," as Dickstein notes.[77] Yet Dickstein probably ascribes too much newness to the New Criticism. One could equally argue that what the New Critics set aside was never essential to literary scholarship in the first place—certainly never as essential as contextual considera-tions were, and continue to be, for biblical scholarship—so that the New Criticism represented a distillation and intensification of what was cen-tral and indispensable to the older literary scholarship rather than an absolute or even radical break with it.

In any case, with the New Critical reformulation, literary scholar-ship effectively returned to its origins in "pre-critical" biblical com-mentary. With the New Critical blinkers balanced on his nose to filter out every "extrinsic" distraction and commune uninterruptedly with a mystified literary Word, the literary critic turned back the critical clock and transformed scholarship once again into *lectio divina*. The doc-trine of *sola scriptura* became a doctrine of *sola litteratura*. Given the raw affinity of the New Criticism with pre-critical biblical exegesis, it is hardly surprising that even when it was at the height of its influence and allure in Anglo-American literary studies, it was thoroughly ignored by biblical scholars, perhaps instinctively; for biblical scholars have always regarded the pre-critical interpreter as their constitutive other.

---

76. According to Dickstein (ibid., 62), who himself had taken Wellek's class.
77. Ibid.

With the rise of the New Criticism, the literary "scholar" mutated into the literary "critic." Academic literary study became an affair of "unmediated" and intimate engagement with the literary artifact that set all previously distracting concern for "background" aside. Biblical scholars, in contrast, even today, tend to refer to themselves as biblical "critics" just as infrequently as literary critics refer to themselves as literary "scholars." Biblical scholars continue to labour under the imperative to mark themselves *as* scholars. Whereas literary critics after the New Criticism could think unrestrainedly in terms of unmediated, immanentist, intimate reading, biblical scholars had to continue, self-consciously and emphatically, to separate what they did from a Protestant-Romantic, pious communion with the text. Their work had to be clearly marked *as* work—as other than the subjective, self-indulgent, personal, private, pietistic, devotional, pastoral, homiletical, or confessional. Their work had to seem productive; it had to talk in terms of yield, adding to the cumulative sum of knowledge in the field. Most of all, it had to mark its constitutive difference from naïve lay-reading by setting up protective barriers of specialization.

This brand of biblical scholarship had its ultimate roots in classical scholarship. The early eighteenth century saw the invention of a specialist philology centered on the microscopic textual analysis of classical Greek and Latin literature—"on vain Niceties and captious Cavils, about Words and Syllables," as one unimpressed contemporary put it.[78] The birth of the professional philologist marked a general shift in English letters from a "gentlemanly humanism" to an expert enterprise, and from an ethos of appreciation to an ethos of criticism.[79] England's leading classical scholar, Richard Bentley, was at the vanguard of this transformation. In 1716, however, Bentley began to turn his critical gaze to the Greek New Testament. Under his influence and that of his contemporary John Mill, microscopic philology began to dominate biblical scholarship.[80] Its initial purpose was to reclaim the Bible from

78. William Temple, "Some Thoughts upon Reviewing the Essay of Ancient and Modern Learning," in *Works* (London, 1720), Vol. 1, 299, quoted in Sheehan, *The Enlightenment Bible*, 46.

79. See Sheehan, *The Enlightenment Bible*, 46, and Simon Jarvis, *Scholars and Gentlemen: Shakespearean Textual Criticism and Representations of Scholarly Labour, 1725–1765* (Oxford: Clarendon, 1995), 21.

80. See Sheehan, *The Enlightenment Bible*, 46–47.

the monster that the Reformation had unleashed—the "intellectually unwashed" and undisciplined mass-reader able to read the Bible in the vernacular and hence to read into it anything and everything that "spirit," "conscience," or readerly whim might dictate.[81] If Protestantism ostensibly represented the removal of priestly mediation and the opening up of the Word to the "common man," the proliferation of technical biblical scholarship provided a new kind of authoritative mediation. An elite class of accredited experts now ringed about the biblical text, guarding it from the undisciplined lay reader.

The habit of esotericism, once securely reestablished, would prove difficult to break. Scholars would continue to churn out arcane discourse on and around the Bible long after they had forgotten why they first began to do so. (In contemporary societies as secularized as that of Great Britain, say, it is exceedingly easy to forget. Avid Bible readers of any stripe, whether expert or "naive," orthodox or heretical, are now vying with the harbor porpoise and the native dormouse for inclusion on the list of protected species.) Even as the reasons for such discourse receded, however, the incentives for engaging in it increased, the discipline gradually developing elaborate internal incitements and deterrents to preserve and perpetuate its esoteric character. In contemporary academic culture, these incentives and disincentives achieve quintessential expression in the policy, common to all the "better" universities, colleges, and seminaries, of valuing scholarly monographs over books written for the general public, and technical articles in peer-reviewed journals over articles in periodicals with a broad circulation, in matters of hiring, tenure, and promotion. Even as the general public has become less and less interested in what the professional biblical scholar has to say, the profession has become more and more interested in ensuring that the biblical scholar spend less and less time addressing himself or herself to the general public.

And the situation is likely to get worse before it gets better—or simply get worse and worse. The recent divorce of the American Academy of Religion and the Society of Biblical Literature, whereby the two societies now no longer share hotel rooms and meeting space for their annual conferences, will likely have the effect of causing SBL to turn in on itself

---

81. Cf. Ibid., 48.

even more.[82] During the honeymoon years, the two societies snuggled up to each other in the joint program book, the AAR program laid out on every left-hand page of the book in intimate proximity to the SBL program laid out on every right-hand page.[83] In consequence, even the most incestuously intradisciplinary biblical specialist, venturing into the program book to discover the venue of, say, the morning session of the Corpus Hellenisticum Novi Testamenti program unit, could not fail to register, at least in his peripheral vision, the expansive vistas of the AAR program over the horizon of the SBL page, and run the risk of sudden intellectual vertigo.

Cable television would have us believe that biblical scholarship is an enterprise dedicated to the deciphering of secrets: *Mysteries of the Bible*; *The Bible's Buried Secrets*; *Cracking the Bible Code*. . . . First and foremost, however, biblical scholarship is itself a secret, or secretive, enterprise. But what is it that biblical experts secretly discuss amongst themselves, cloistered behind the locked doors of the technical journal and the scholarly monograph? The answer is that they debate the *problems* of the biblical text. For the evangelical Christian, the Bible is a book of solutions. ("Reverend Graham, backsliding has always been a problem for me. Where in the Bible can I find help with it?" "Friend, you only need to read Psalm 51, followed by 1 John 1:4-9.") For the biblical scholar, in contrast, the Bible is a book of problems—the Synoptic Problem;[84] the problem of evil in the Hebrew Bible; the problem of theodicy in the deuteronomistic history; Acts and the problem of genre; Pastorals and the problem of pseudonymity; the problem of historicity in books

---

82. Cf. R. S. Sugirtharajah, "Muddling Along at the Margins," in *Still at the Margins: Biblical Scholarship Fifteen Years after the Voices from the Margin*, ed. R. S. Sugirtharajah (New York: T. & T. Clark International, 2008), 18.

83. The redesign of the program book in 2001 so that the entire AAR program occupied the first half of the book and the entire SBL program the second half may be read in hindsight as an early sign of cracks in the marriage and a retreat to separate bedrooms.

84. The Problem of biblical problems, the one that merits capital letters. Werner Georg Kümmel in the chapter on the Problem in his classic introduction to the New Testament (a chapter that fairly wallows in the Problem, emblazoning the word "Problem" not just in its main title but also in each of its section titles: "The Synoptic Problem"; "The Problem"; "The History of the Synoptic Problem"; "Attempt at a Solution to the Synoptic Problem") dismisses out of the hand the notion that Augustine or any other pre-critical exegete properly grasped that there even *was* a problem. "The real problem was first recognized in the second half of the eighteenth century" (*Introduction to the New Testament* [17th ed.; trans. Howard Clark Kee; Nashville: Abingdon, 1975], 44).

too numerous to list. . . . Like textual errors—as opposed to "moral" errors—such problems are not only necessary but positively welcome. Nor are they hard to find. Indeed, it is almost as though the Bible had been composed precisely with the professional needs of the modern biblical scholar in mind. As Jacques Berlinerblau remarks, "composition by aggregate has spawned a chaotic, sprawling, disjointed anthology, overflowing with meanings and meaninglessness, blinking neon light contradictions, ambiguities, ellipses, and numbing repetition."[85] In a carefully circumscribed but infinitely proliferating sense, errors, conundrums, and *cruces interpretum* are the bread-and-butter of the biblical studies industry.

In this respect, as in many others, the orthodox and the heterodox lie uncannily close together. Polemic against the so-called "Deists" castigated them for conjuring up spurious biblical problems. An anti-Deist broadside of 1677 complained that they "hunt up and down the *Scriptures* for every thing that seems a difficulty . . . and then by heaping all these together . . . make the *Scriptures* seem a confused heap of indigested stuff."[86] But the insistent positing of problems in the biblical text also became the incipient gesture of orthodox biblical scholarship and remains the signal trait of the biblical professional, even if he or she has long since learned to gesture more politely to these problems and to place himself or herself on the side of their solution, albeit indefinitely deferred. Perhaps the principal difference between the Bible's perceived guardians or destroyers lies not in the perception of problems but in the tone in which those problems are raised. If problems sometimes provided a kind of savage joy for the "Deists," they are also, in a real sense, a delight to the biblical scholar, for the whole point about problems is that they require professional expertise.

Formative biblical criticism reinvented the Bible as a potentially limitless compendium of conundrums and obscurities awaiting solution—the kind of solution that only the professional biblical critic was qualified to propose. Fortunately for the biblical scholar (who, after all, needs job security as much as any professional), most of these problems, and most

---

85. Jacques Berlinerblau, *The Secular Bible: Why Nonbelievers Must Take the Bible Seriously* (Cambridge: Cambridge University Press, 2005), 62.

86. Edward Stillingfleet, *A Letter to a Deist, in Answer to Several Objections against the Truth and Authority of the Scriptures* (London, 1677), 9, quoted in Sheehan, *The Enlightenment Bible*, 38.

especially the larger ones, are precisely the sort that do not admit of final solution. Is there any article title more reassuringly familiar to the consumer of biblical-scholarly journals than the one that begins "Once Again: The Problem of . . ."? Long before we have established the sources of the Pentateuch, say, or the literary interrelationships of the Synoptic Gospels in ways acceptable to every expert in the field, the very questions that ignited the entire enterprise of source criticism will have become as moot as such self-evidently momentous earlier questions as whether the allegorical sense of Scripture needs the literal sense or not.

In a certain sense, then, "Post-Theory" is a Theory "yet to come."[1]

[N]o post, no postism, no post-theory can be sheared away from the question and experience of *déjà vu*.[2]

ONWARD
TOWARD
THE
PAST

I. Theory in the First Wave:
When Historical Critics Ruled the Earth
The Biblical Sub-Sub-Sub-Specialist

The history of the diffuse yet circumscribed Enlightenment Bible helps to explain what did and did not, could and could not, happen in the first engagement between the Bible and Theory. That encounter took place largely within the parameters of the Enlightenment Bible. As we saw earlier, the Enlightenment Bible was the product of a ceaseless task of pluralization and dissemination across ever-proliferating spheres of investigation. This frenetic activity yielded amoeba-like splitting and self-propagation—specialization, sub-specialization, and sub-sub-specialialization. The first major split occurred with the Great Testamentary Divide: beginning in the early nineteenth century, biblical scholars began to self-identify either as "Old Testament scholars" or "New Testament scholars."[3] By the latter half of the twentieth century, the disciplinary tank was brimming with squirming, self-multiplying micro-organisms. At a certain moment in the evolutionary process, for instance, the "Markan scholar" was born. Then the "Markan literary critic"; that is, the professional, perhaps prolific, biblical scholar all of whose published oeuvre—spanning, even, an entire career—was devoted to literary readings of Mark's twenty pages: a subspecialist in a subdiscipline of a subdiscipline.

Methodology was the medium of this subdisciplinary splitting: redaction criticism splits off from form criticism, then structuralism splits off from both form and redaction criticism, while poststructuralism splits off from structuralism even as narrative criticism splits off from redaction criticism. And each new method brings an entire new set of *problems* into view: the Synoptic Problem is not a problem at all for the structuralist, but the fine-tuning of an actantial model adequate to the complexities of biblical narrative, or some other equally arcane challenge, *is* a pressing problem for him or her. Scholars exhausted with endlessly wringing out tired old problems and tweaking tired old solutions could acquire

---

1. Martin McQuillan, Graeme MacDonald, Robin Purves, and Stephen Thomson, "The Joy of Theory," in *Post-Theory: New Directions in Criticism*, ed. Martin McQuillan et al. (Edinburgh: Edinburgh University Press, 1999), xv.

2. Nicholas Royle, "Déjà Vu," in McQuillan et al., *Post-Theory*, 4.

3. See Gerald Bray, *Biblical Interpretation: Past and Present* (Downers Grove, Ill.: InterVarsity, 1996), 274.

entire new research agendas simply by switching methods. Through such shifts they could also multiply exponentially the amount of primary text on which they could authoritatively pronounce. No longer would a doctoral dissertation or scholarly article need to be limited to a single theme or passage—if not a single verse—due to the crippling quantity of secondary literature dragging in its wake. One could blithely set aside all manner of fatigued and fatiguing projects—*Deuteronomic Curse Forms Reconsidered*, say, or "Once Again: Baking Bread on Human Dung (Ezekiel 4:12)"—to pursue pioneering projects that sounded impossibly ambitious yet were eminently manageable, due to the (temporary) paucity of secondary literature—*Queering the Minor Prophets*, for instance, or *Feminism, Deconstruction, and the Bible (with the Apocrypha and Pseudepigrapha)*. The more heavily populated the field of biblical studies became, and the older and more jaded the inherited research paradigms became, the more methods were needed to go around and ensure that everybody had enough important new problems and a big enough patch of primary text on which to exercise their unique expertise. Methodological know-how was the biblical professional's identity badge; it was what distinguished him or her from the common or garden-variety Bible reader. The reinvention of the Bible in the eighteenth century as a book of problems necessitated the invention of the biblical professional, and vice versa, while methodology was designed as the new hermeneutical key.

This was the professional ethos to which Theory had to be accommodated on its entry into the discipline. Theory, in the form of a banalized and sloganized postmodernism, was translated into biblical studies as an exhortation to overhaul and refuel the aged methodological engine of the discipline. Theory in this perhaps inevitably narrowed form extended, rather than challenged, the fundamental project of the Enlightenment Bible—however much anti-Enlightenment polemic might feature in biblical postmodernist rhetoric. (Habermas's "Modernity—An Incomplete Project" was required reading for biblical postmodernists in the 1980s, but generally only as a foil for Lyotard and other Theorists for whom the preferred tool for reflecting on the Enlightenment legacy was a sledgehammer rather than a chisel.)[4]

---

4. Jürgen Habermas, "Modernity—An Incomplete Project," in *The Anti-Aesthetic: Essays on Postmodern Culture*, ed. Hal Foster (Seattle: Bay Press, 1983), 3–15; Jean-François Lyotard, *The Postmodern Condition: A Report on Knowledge* (trans. Geoff Bennington and Brian Massumi; Minneapolis: University of Minnesota Press, 1984).

Reader-response criticism, "deconstructionism," ideological criticism, and other vaguely postmodernist "-isms" helped to meet the intensified demand for new methods and approaches caused by wear and tear (through overuse) on the old historical-critical machine.

Once biblical studies methodology, however, is subjected to an intensification and acceleration of supply and demand, the road to obsolescence and irrelevance can become dismayingly short. A method's or "approach's" heroic age can give way with disconcerting rapidity to a rather less glorious phase in which the critic finds himself or herself not so much standing on the shoulders of giants as sorting through their trash. Queer theory in biblical studies, for instance, can be said to have achieved heroic dimensions in 2006 with the publication of the 859-page *Queer Bible Commentary*, a Brobdingnagian volume for a Herculean labor: that of queering all sixty-six books of the Bible (even those containing no whiff whatsoever of sexual activity).[5] In literary studies, meanwhile, a mere two decades after the dazzling debut of queer theory in that discipline, critics seem to be running out of texts and things to queer. *Queering Cold War Poetry*, anyone?[6]

Political Theory

Hand-in-hand with the "Theorization"—more precisely, the "poststructuralization"—of literary studies during the past thirty years or so has gone a "politicization" of literary studies. The latter began in no small part, indeed, as a reaction against the former, a backlash against the perceived apoliticism of early American deconstruction, in particular, of the late 1970s and early 1980s.[7] This political reaction, however, while

---

5. Deryn Guest, Robert E. Goss, Mona West, and Thomas Bohache, eds., *The Queer Bible Commentary* (London: SCM, 2006). One unintended lesson this volume teaches, indeed, is that when even a hint of sex is absent from the biblical material, queer commentary can tend, for many pages at a time, to sound drearily indistinguishable from straight commentary (although it need not, as certain of the more resourceful commentators manage to demonstrate).

6. Eric Keenaghan, *Queering Cold War Poetry: Ethics of Vulnerability in Cuba and the United States* (Columbus: The Ohio State University Press, 2009).

7. Two influential expressions of this backlash were Edward W. Said, "The Problem of Textuality: Two Exemplary Positions," *Critical Inquiry* 4 (1978): 673–714, which pitted a politicized Foucault against a depoliticized Derrida, and Frank Lentricchia, *After the New Criticism* (Chicago: University of Chicago Press, 1980), a trenchant critique of deconstructive "formalism" (epitomized for Lentricchia by Paul de Man, as we noted earlier).

frequently shouldering poststructuralism aside altogether, has more often tended to harness it instead for the analysis of an incrementally expanding set of social, cultural, and historical phenomena: gender and sexuality; race and ethnicity; colonialism, postcolonialism, and neocolonialism; and, most recently, as we have seen, human interaction with the non-human world. Poststructuralism and the political have forged potent fusions in critical phenomena ranging from cultural studies, New Historicism, and gender studies to postcolonial studies, queer studies, and posthuman animality studies—which is to say in virtually every high-profile "movement" in literary studies since the heyday of "Yale deconstruction" in the late 1970s and early 1980s. The politicization of U.S. literary studies has, however, been even more pervasive than its poststructuralization. This politicization preceded poststructuralism in the U.S. academy in the forms of Marxist and especially feminist criticisms, and even at present, in a post-post-everything age of jaded appetite and outright exhaustion, shows no signs of abating. More even than generic poststructuralism, it remains the untranscendable horizon in contemporary literary studies to the extent that it seems at present all but impossible to imagine what might possibly succeed it as the dominant intellectual ethos of the discipline.[8]

Biblical studies too, of course, although certainly in a less concerted fashion than literary studies, has veered increasingly into the political in recent decades. All in all, however, literary studies has provided little direct impetus for this swerve in biblical studies. Notable political developments in literary studies, such as New Historicism, postcolonial studies, and queer studies, have only been taken up in biblical studies since the mid-1990s or later, and remain on the fringes of the field. Feminist biblical criticism and other liberationist enterprises in hermeneutics and exegesis—not least, liberation theology and hermeneutics themselves—have more directly catalyzed the political turn in biblical studies. Emblematic of that turn was Elisabeth Schüssler Fiorenza's landmark presidential address to the Society of Biblical Literature in 1987 on "The Ethics of Biblical Interpretation."[9] Schüssler Fiorenza's

---

8. The Sisyphean (and somewhat reactionary) efforts of Stanley Fish notwithstanding. See, for example, his *Save the World on Your Own Time* (Oxford: Oxford University Press, 2008).

9. Elisabeth Schüssler Fiorenza, "The Ethics of Biblical Interpretation: Decentering Biblical Scholarship," *Journal of Biblical Literature* 107:1 (1988): 3–17.

accession as a leading feminist biblical scholar to the presidency of SBL, coupled with her courageous presidential address, which challenged biblical scholars to engage "the ethical consequences and political functions of biblical texts in their historical as well as in their contemporary sociopolitical contexts,"[10] signaled at least a temporary movement to the center of the discipline of what had formerly been peripheral to it. Poststructuralism, however—already emblematic of extra-biblical literary studies when Schüssler Fiorenza delivered her address—remained in the margins, Schüssler Fiorenza's distrust of malestream historical criticism being coupled with a concomitant distrust of postmodernism in general and poststructuralism in particular.[11] Schüssler Fiorenza's SBL presidency thus signified something instructively different than J. Hillis Miller's MLA presidency of the previous year, the latter being widely billed as signaling "the triumph of theory" (read: poststructuralism) in literary studies—not least because that very expression was brazenly emblazoned in the title of his presidential address.[12] In short, whereas a self-consciously political stance has frequently, even regularly, gone hand-in-hand with poststructuralism in literary studies in recent decades, their conjunction in biblical studies has been far more the exception than the rule.[13]

---

10. Ibid., 15. "If scriptural texts have served not only noble causes but also to legitimate war, to nurture anti-Judaism and misogynism, to justify the exploitation of slavery, and to promote colonial dehumanization . . . then the responsibility of the biblical scholar cannot be restricted to giving the readers of our time clear access to the original intentions of the biblical writers" (ibid.).

11. For detailed discussion of Schüssler Fiorenza's stance on postmodernism, see The Bible and Culture Collective, *The Postmodern Bible* (New Haven, Conn.: Yale University Press, 1995), 260–67.

12. J. Hillis Miller, "The Triumph of Theory, the Resistance to Reading, and the Question of the Material Base," *PMLA* 102 (1987):281–91.

13. Fusions of feminism and deconstruction constitute one set of exceptions; see, for example, Stephen D. Moore, *Poststructuralism and the New Testament: Derrida and Foucault at the Foot of the Cross* (Minneapolis: Fortress Press, 1994), 43–64; Yvonne M. Sherwood, *The Prostitute and the Prophet: Hosea's Marriage in Literary-Theoretical Perspective* (Journal for the Study of the Old Testament Supplement Series, 212; Sheffield: Sheffield Academic, 1996; reprinted as *The Prostitute and the Prophet: Reading Hosea in the Late Twentieth Century* [London: T. & T. Clark, 2004]); Gary A. Phillips, "The Ethics of Reading Deconstructively, or Speaking Face-to-Face: The Samaritan Woman Meets Derrida at the Well," in *The New Literary Criticism of the New Testament*, ed. Elizabeth Struthers Malbon and Edgar McKnight (Sheffield: Sheffield Academic, 1994), 283–325; David Rutledge, *Reading Marginally: Feminism, Deconstruction and the Bible* (Biblical Interpretation Series, 21; Leiden: Brill, 1996); and certain of the essays in Yvonne Sherwood, ed., *Derrida's Bible: Reading a Page of Scripture with a Little Help from Derrida*

The Dirt on Politics

We feel compelled, however, to point out, albeit in fear and trembling, that *politics* and *the political* are thoroughly mystified terms in much contemporary academic discourse (including the previous two paragraphs of the present work). Only consider that *politics*, in particular, is a term that, in the extra-academic world, so regularly and spontaneously combines on the tongue with certain other terms— "crooked," "corrupt," "dirty," "shady," "unscrupulous," "backroom," "bankrupt," "partisan," "hypocritical," "failed," and so on—as to render "the political" less a synonym of "the ethical" than its virtual antonym. Within the hermetic enclosure of academic literary studies, in contrast, and even within that of academic biblical studies—at any rate those sectors of it not dominated by old-school historical criticism[14]—to claim the term "political" for one's work is implicitly to claim the moral high ground and a nimbus of virtue ("In my recent trilogy on Haggai, I'm attempting to revive and retool form criticism for explicitly *political* work . . . "), while failure on the part of others to claim that term and terrain is just as regularly construed as the mark of a (possibly moral) lack ("Allow me to pose the 'so what?' question, if I may. What would you say are the *political* implications of your—admittedly intriguing— interpretation of the phrase 'unnatural lust' in the Letter of Jude?").

The Society of Biblical Literature's annual conference is, in any case, a rather peculiar venue for self-consciously political forms of biblical criticism, whether mystified or not. A certain surreality, indeed, nec- essarily attends the presentation of such criticism in such a context, most of all when the politics involved are radical. Only consider that the

---

(New York: Palgrave Macmillan, 2004). Certain of David Jobling's early essays engage in broader mergings of deconstruction and the political; see, for example, "Writing the Wrongs of the World: The Deconstruction of the Biblical Text in the Context of Lib- eration Theologies," *Semeia* 51 (1990): 81–118, and "Deconstruction and the Political Analysis of Biblical Texts: A Jamesonian Reading of Psalm 72," *Semeia* 59 (1992): 95–127. Foucauldian readings constitute yet another set of exceptions; see, for example, Eliz- abeth A. Castelli, *Imitating Paul: A Discourse of Power* (Literary Currents in Biblical Interpretation; Louisville, Ky.: Westminster John Knox, 1991); Stephen D. Moore, *God's Gym: Divine Male Bodies of the Bible* (London and New York: Routledge, 1996), 1–34; and Sandra Hack Polaski, *Paul and the Discourse of Power* (Sheffield: Sheffield Academic, 1999). And certain engagements with postcolonial theory constitute yet another set; see pp. 37–38 nn. 102–3 above.

14. Those sectors, that is, in which the terms "politics" and "the political" are scru- pulously reserved for the remote past—the politics of ancient Israel, say, or those of the Judean temple-state.

presenter is almost invariably doomed to read his or her neo-Marxist analysis of Micah or Mark in a room with a name like "The Boardroom" or "Ballroom B," itself situated in a luxury hotel in a well-heeled neighborhood of a "culture-rich" or tourist-attractive North American city,[15] and that the only member of the underclass likely to be in earshot will be the hotel employee sent in to replenish the iced water.

Postmodernism, too, it must be said, has hindered as well as helped the "political" in the context of the Society of Biblical Literature. Notwithstanding its iconoclastic hammers, polemical knives, and other alarming accessories, biblical postmodernism seems rather helpfully to underwrite the often trite tolerance and relativism that is another mainstay of the biblical studies discipline: "Let many flowers bloom," or "You in your small corner and I in mine." This ethos of enable-and-ignore is what ensures both that postmodernism is allotted its own program units in the SBL annual meeting and that these program units and those allotted to old-school historical criticism (very many more, to be sure) constitute, in combination, a textbook example of the mathematical phenomenon known as "disjoint sets"—two sets, that is, that have no members in common. A cynic might remark that this mutual indifference is precisely what prevents biblical studies from coming apart altogether at the seams and disintegrating into cacophonous incommensurability; it enables us all to coexist peaceably if not comfortably. But there are certain costs that arise from this arrangement, as we began to see in the previous chapter.

Terry Eagleton worries aloud that academic themes of plurality, difference, and even transgression dovetail all too seamlessly with Western capitalism and its anethical ethic of endless consumer choice.[16] Other critics, such as Herman Rapaport and Amanda Anderson, have reflected on the mutual indifference that results from construing all critical positions as merely perspectival or effects of identity (cultural, racial/ethnic, gender, sexual, etc.), reducing the force of argument and

---

15. Of cities selected for (AAR/)SBL in recent decades, Kansas City (1991) came closest to being the rule-proving exception. Acute disgruntlement with the venue among the attendees ensured that the conference has not returned there. The list of populous U.S. cities (never mind Canadian) in which it would be more or less impossible to imagine SBL meeting even once would run in the hundreds, ranging from Newark, New Jersey, to Oakland, California, and from Flint, Michigan, to Brownsville, Texas.

16. Terry Eagleton, *After Theory* (New York: Basic, 2003), 20–21.

eliminating the necessity of confronting and working through critical, ideological, philosophical, and theological divisions.[17] To date, however, such concerns have barely begun to be voiced from within biblical studies (we return to this issue below), even though our particular disciplinary history, which has imprinted us with a voracious appetite for method, has made us particularly susceptible to the atomized indifference of what Rapaport dubs the "approach approach."[18] In the rhetoric of the postmodernist critique of mainstream biblical scholarship—and also that of the currently proliferating readings of biblical texts from different "social locations"—the challenge of the particular as opposed to the universal has been voiced as a radical challenge to the discipline's traditional belief in universal and homogenized relevance. In practice, however, the rise of fragmentation and particularism, while often bewailed by traditionalists, has emerged smoothly out of the imperative encoded from the outset in the Enlightenment Bible: to be fruitful and multiply methodologically.

The Dirt on Biblical Scholars

Theory has also been readily absorbed in other more specific ways as a relatively painless extension of work-as-usual in biblical studies. Insistence on the material, social, and political contexts of literature, for instance, (re)emerging in earnest in literary studies in the 1980s, tended to grate on the sensibilities of older literary critics whose approach to literature was still oriented by New Critical principles. Such insistence, however, in the abstract at least, would hardly raise eyebrows among traditionally minded biblical scholars. The assertion that *The Tempest* cannot be legitimately separated from issues of colonialism and imperialism may seem a travesty of Shakespearean criticism to some; but biblical scholars were already busily reading biblical texts against the backdrop of empire while Stephen Greenblatt and the other New Historicist Shakespeareans were still in short pants. (One important reason, indeed, why empire studies has recently taken off in such a

---

17. Herman Rapaport, *The Theory Mess: Deconstruction in Eclipse* (New York: Columbia University Press, 2001), 155 and throughout; Amanda Anderson, *The Way We Argue Now: A Study in the Cultures of Theory* (Princeton, N.J.: Princeton University Press, 2006), 5.

18. Rapaport, *The Theory Mess*, 155.

big way in New Testament studies[19] is that one doesn't actually need to read postcolonial theory, New Historicism, or any other abstruse, headache-inducing work in order to do it. One knows perfectly well how to read Mark or Revelation against the background of empire, thank you, without any outside assistance. One has always been doing it, actually, just not quite as single-mindedly.) The dissolving of literary texts in economic contexts, likewise, does not feel nearly as reductive in a discipline that recognizes the study of ancient coins as one of its legitimate areas of endeavor. Insofar as Theory's import has in part been about earthing in the material, getting oneself dirty up to the elbows in it, it has been anything but a drastic disciplinary break for biblical scholars. Such earthing, such contextualizing, such rubbing of a formerly airy and unearthly text in the mud of history, was also one of the gestures that engendered the Enlightenment Bible.

The Good Book as Great Book

Earlier we noted, following Jonathan Sheehan, how the Enlightenment Bible was also the Cultural Bible, theological authority having been translated into cultural authority, and the Bible having been rehabilitated as the "foundation of (Western) culture" and hence a legitimate object of cultural inquiry. The incursions of Theory (in this case, literary theory) in biblical studies have also been on a continuum with this aspect of the Enlightenment Bible, reiterating and updating the mantra of the Bible's cultural authority—indeed, cultural inescapability. Biblical literary criticism, in some of its more hyperbolic manifestations, has taken the form of deflected worship, a translation of the sacred into the aesthetic. Eagleton describes the belle-lettristic world of literary criticism before Theory as one in which "fulsome vocabulary" such as "remarkably fine," "splendidly robust," or "drearily naturalistic" was "ruthlessly superimposed on every work."[20] But biblical literary criticism has strayed into the cosmic reaches of the hyperbolic on occasion, and generally eschewed negative evaluations of any kind. Northrop Frye, for instance, famously prostrated himself before a Bible that seemed to

---

19. For an overview, see Stephen D. Moore, "Paul after Empire," in *The Colonized Apostle: Paul and Postcolonial Studies*, ed. Christopher D. Stanley (Paul in Critical Contexts; Minneapolis: Fortress Press, forthcoming).

20. Eagleton, *After Theory*, 94.

loom massively in the midst of Western culture, "frustrating all attempts to walk around it"; while Robert Alter has, more recently, made the gargantuan claim that the Bible "seizes the imagination of the modern writer because of his acute consciousness of it as . . . one of the primary possibilities of representing the human condition and . . . historical experience for all the eras of Western culture."[21] Sheehan marvels that such extravagant statements have become so normative that we scarcely notice them any longer.[22]

This notion of the Bible not just as Good Book but as Great Book is at once a high-cultural and low-cultural cliché, a fact of which the Republican presidential primary debate hosted by CNN and YouTube in November 2007 served to remind the American electorate. The only dramatic moment in an otherwise dull debate occurred when a rather intense young man, beamed in remotely by video link from Dallas, Texas, challenged the presidential hopefuls: "How you answer this question will tell us everything we need to know about you. Do you believe every word of this book? Specifically, this book that I am holding in my hand. *Do you believe this book?*" The book was, of course, a Bible, and the questioner punctuated his challenge by thrusting it repeatedly into the camera. The question, naturally enough, elicited a series of squirmingly evasive replies. "I think it's the greatest book ever written," former New York mayor Rudy Giuliani ventured, feeling for uncontroversial ground, and finding it. His statement elicited applause from the audience. Not just the Good Book and a Great Book, then, but the Greatest Book of all. That the Bible is the Masterpiece of literary masterpieces is a theological statement masquerading as a cultural statement. It is hardly surprising, therefore, that Alter's *The Art of Biblical Narrative* has been the best-received foray to date by a "secular" literary critic into biblical studies.[23] What better confirmation of the legitimacy of an academic

---

21. Northrop Frye, *The Great Code: The Bible and Literature* (London: Routledge and Kegan Paul, 1982), cover notes; Robert Alter, *Canon and Creativity: Modern Writing and the Authority of Scripture* (New Haven, Conn.: Yale University Press, 2000), 17–18.

22. Jonathan Sheehan, *The Enlightenment Bible: Translation, Scholarship, Culture* (Princeton, N.J.: Princeton University Press, 2004), x.

23. Robert Alter, *The Art of Biblical Narrative* (New York: Basic, 1983). Steven Weitzman observes: "By the most conventional measures—number of books sold, favorable reviews, frequency of citation—it is hard to imagine a more successful academic book than Alter's . . ." ("Before and After *The Art of Biblical Narrative*," *Prooftexts* 27 [2007]: 196).

discipline centered solely on the Bible could be imagined than a work by a distinguished outsider that celebrates the Bible as the Book of books—and ostensibly on literary rather than theological grounds, so that it is as much a book of the academy as of the church or synagogue?

For the project of the Enlightenment Bible to be faithfully continued and fully realized, however, the Bible must be shown to be not just a book that properly belongs in the academy but one that permeates Western culture at large. To this end, historical criticism and literary criticism of the Bible have needed to be supplemented by cultural studies. Theory, on entering biblical studies, this time under the rubric of cultural studies, is once again pulled into orbit around the Enlightenment Bible. The mantra of the Bible as the book that Western culture cannot get over or get around finds its consummate expression in biblical cultural studies, whether through analysis of the biblical in the paintings of Rembrandt, William Blake, or Samuel Bak; operatic libretto, Bach's cantatas, or the lyrics of U2; *The Passion of the Christ* or *The Life of Brian*; or the political rhetoric of Margaret Thatcher or George W. Bush.[24] The invention of

---

24. To cite a handful of examples from what is now an extensive body of scholarly literature. See, respectively, Mieke Bal, *Reading Rembrandt: Beyond the Word-Image Opposition* (Cambridge: Cambridge University Press, 1991; 2nd ed.: Amsterdam: Amsterdam University Press, 2006); Christopher Rowland, *Wheels within Wheels: William Blake and Ezekiel's Merkabah in Text and Image* (Milwaukee, Wis.: Marquette University Press, 2007); Gary A. Phillips, Danna Nolan Fewell, and Yvonne Sherwood, eds., *Representing the Irreparable: The Shoah, the Bible, and the Art of Samuel Bak* (Boston: Pucker Art Publications; Syracuse: Syracuse University Press, 2008); Helen Leneman, *The Performed Bible: The Story of Ruth in Opera and Oratorio* (The Bible in the Modern World, 11; Sheffield: Sheffield Phoenix, 2007); John Rogerson, "The Use of the Song of Songs in J. S. Bach's Church Cantatas," in *Biblical Studies/Cultural Studies: The Third Sheffield Colloquium*, ed. J. Cheryl Exum and Stephen D. Moore (Gender, Culture, Theory, 7; Sheffield: Sheffield Academic, 1998), 343–51; Andrew C. Dowsett, "Cuts," in *In Search of the Present: The Bible through Cultural Studies*, ed. Stephen D. Moore (Semeia, 82; Atlanta: Society of Biblical Literature, 1998), 247–80; Kathleen E. Corley and Robert L. Webb, eds., *Jesus and Mel Gibson's* The Passion of the Christ: *The Film, the Gospels and the Claims of History* (New York: Continuum, 2004); Philip R. Davies, "Life of Brian Research," in Exum and Moore, *Biblical Studies/Cultural Studies*, 400–414; Richard Griffiths, "Mrs. Thatcher's Bible," in Moore, *In Search of the Present*, 99–126; Erin Runions, "Desiring War: Apocalypse, Commodity Fetish, and the End of History," in *The Postcolonial Biblical Reader*, ed. R. S. Sugirtharajah (Oxford: Blackwell, 2006), 112–28; Yvonne Sherwood, "Bush's Bible as a Liberal Bible (Strange Though That Might Seem)," *Postscripts: Sacred Texts and Contemporary Worlds* 2 (2006): 47–58; James G. Crossley, *Jesus in an Age of Terror: Scholarly Projects for a New American Century* (BibleWorld; London: Equinox, 2008). As will be apparent from this list, the present authors, too, have not been able to resist the seductions of the Cultural Bible.

the Enlightenment Bible was facilitated through the emergence of new media and discursive spaces, such as newspapers, encyclopedias, and coffeehouses.[25] Biblical cultural studies extends the encyclopedic dispersion of the Enlightenment Bible, fueled by printer's ink and caffeine, into the age of film, television, cyberspace and hypertext (the contemporary update of the encyclopedia), postmodern art, and kitsch. While few contemporary approaches in biblical studies seem as removed from historical criticism as cultural studies, the latter is arguably as locked as the former into the Enlightenment project of biblical studies—the mission to ensure that the Bible remains relevant to the modern age.

Biblical cultural studies is close to historical criticism in another respect as well, as will gradually become clear in what follows. There is one constitutive difference between biblical cultural studies and "secular" cultural studies. The latter entails a radical and fundamental displacement of the literary canon from the center of critical activity. By the time cultural studies caught on in the U.S. literary academy it already had a thirty-year history in tow.[26] American cultural studies has frequently been castigated for jettisoning the Marxist underpinnings of its formative British phase.[27] Even domesticated and defanged, however, cultural studies may still turn out to have been the most momentous shift of all in U.S. literary studies. For however radical other brands of criticism may appear to be, "literature," however conceived or reconceived, remains

---

25. On the important role of the coffeehouse in creating new communities of discourse, see Brian Cowan, *The Social Life of Coffee: The Emergence of the British Coffeehouse* (New Haven, Conn.: Yale University Press, 2005).

26. A history that, according to the standard recital, began in Britain in the 1950s. For a potted version of that history, see Stephen D. Moore, "Between Birmingham and Jerusalem: Cultural Studies and Biblical Studies," *Semeia* 82 (1998): esp. 3–13. For the unabridged version, see Graeme Turner, *British Cultural Studies: An Introduction* (3rd ed.; London and New York: Routledge, 2003). Broader introductions to cultural studies include Lawrence Grossberg, Cary Nelson, and Paula Treichler, eds., *Cultural Studies* (London and New York: Routledge, 1992); John Storey, ed., *What Is Cultural Studies? A Reader* (London: Arnold, 1996); Ackbar Abbas and John Nguyet Erni, eds., *Internationalizing Cultural Studies: An Anthology* (Oxford: Blackwell, 2004); Pepi Leistyna, ed., *Cultural Studies: From Theory to Action* (Oxford: Blackwell, 2004); Simon During, ed., *The Cultural Studies Reader* (3rd ed.; London and New York: Routledge, 2007); Chris Barker, *Cultural Studies: Theory and Practice* (3rd ed.; London: Sage, 2008); and Michael Ryan, ed., *Cultural Studies: An Anthology* (Oxford: Blackwell, 2008).

27. See Moore, "Between Birmingham and Jerusalem," pp. 17–18, for a catena of quotations from the castigators. See further Ted Striphas, *Cultural Studies: The Institutionalization of Cultural Studies* (London and New York: Routledge, 1998).

their object of analysis. Deconstructionists read Shelley, Proust, and Joyce; postcolonial critics read Conrad, Kipling, and Chinua Achebe; queer theorists read E. M. Forster and Jean Genet; while New Historicists read Shakespeare and, well, Shakespeare. Instead of the canonical works of the classic literary canons, however, cultural studies practitioners infamously read just about anything else (contributors to the seminal collection *Cultural Studies*, to cite a prominent example—at 788 pages it is hard to miss—read such topics as AIDS, everyday life, crime fiction, whiteness, pornography, the Book-of-the-Month Club, and *Rambo*; while contributors to *The Cultural Studies Reader* read shopping malls, advertising, sports fans, heavy metal, Iranian television in Los Angeles, and the romance novel).[28] As one recent account of the rise of cultural studies recalls, "rather suddenly, there were few objects in the world that could not be usefully read as texts."[29] What has tended to fill traditionally minded literature professors with dismay or disgust in recent years has been less the spectacle of the best and brightest graduate students pressing the classics of the various literary canons through a Frenchified theoretical shredder than the spectacle of such students now laboring earnestly to decode the semiotics of *American Idol* or the Victoria's Secret catalogue or the lyrics of hip hop or thrash metal.

Or still more ephemeral texts. Few of the sessions at the 2008 MLA convention created as much buzz, apparently, as the panel session on Twitter (entitled "Microblogging: Producing Discourse in 140 Characters or Less"), winning Twitter the designation "hot research topic" from *The Chronicle of Higher Education*.[30] To certain of the more apocalyptic minds among anxious or angry traditionalists, faced with such ephemera, it is not entirely unimaginable that the academic study of the

---

28. See Grossberg, Nelson and Treichler, *Cultural Studies*; During, *The Cultural Studies Reader*.

29. William B. Warner and Clifford Siskin, "Stopping Cultural Studies," *Profession* (2008): 94.

30. http://chronicle.com/news/article/5728/mla-2008-the-last-roundup (accessed May 15, 2009). By the time you read this, Twitter will likely have gone the way of AOL and MySpace and sundry other cyberspace sensations. This, of course, is the problem with (pop-)cultural studies. For a brief time, an article on, say, the apocalyptic subtext of *The X-Files* (see Brenda E. Brasher, "From Revelation to *The X-Files*: An Autopsy of Millennialism in American Popular Culture," in Moore, *In Search of the Present*, 281–95) can make an article on Albrecht Dürer's apocalyptic woodcuts seem stuffy and geriatric; but before long the museum addicts are having the last laugh.

literary canons will gradually become an esoteric discipline, comparable to the study of, say, Old or Middle English in current academic culture. At the very least, literature's place at the centre of "literary studies" can no longer be comfortably assumed.[31]

And even when cultural studies assumes a more serious and sober mien, renouncing the titillating enticements of pop culture for the dry and dusty historical archive—the more common approach to cultural studies, it must be admitted—the literary canons fare no better. Marjorie Perloff gloomily contemplates the following sample:

> At Stanford, of the forty-nine dissertations completed between 2000 and 2006 [in the departments of language and literature], exactly one deals with a single author, Henry James. But it is not just the rejection of the individual author, of "genius theory," that has become *de rigueur*. Of the remaining forty-eight dissertations, only a handful have any specifically literary component. The following are typical titles: "The Garden and the Crop: Revising Rural Labor in the United States Urban Imagination, 1870–1915," "Offending Lives: Subjectivity and Australian Convict Autobiographies, 1788–1899," and "The Sway of Chance in Eighteenth Century England." These dissertations may well use literary texts as examples, but if so, the fictions, dramas, or poems in question are taken to be means to an end—they are windows through which we see the world beyond the text, symptoms of cultural desires, drives, anxieties, or prejudices.[32]

Cultural studies in this "world behind the text" mode, indeed, might well be taken for the lost twin of biblical historical criticism, if it were not for one crucial difference: the latter is joined by an umbilical cord to a canonical body of literature.

---

31. An early testament to this crisis was the "forum" of thirty-two letters on the strained relations between literary studies and cultural studies published in the March 1997 issue of *PMLA*, the MLA's flagship journal.

32. Marjorie Perloff, "Presidential Address 2006: It Must Change," *PMLA* 122 (2007): 654.

In marked contrast to "secular" cultural studies, biblical cultural studies is as tightly tethered to the canon as the historical biblical criticism with which it seems to be so utterly at odds—if not more so: historical critics, at least, like to slum it occasionally in extracanonical texts, but one will search in vain for studies of allusions to *1 Enoch* or the *Gospel of Thomas* in the political speeches of George W. Bush or Barack Obama. Whereas cultural studies seems to imperil the future of literary studies, threatening to knock the disciplinary wheel off its axle, biblical cultural studies, for all its apparent novelty, is entirely continuous with the impulse that gave rise to the biblical studies discipline in the first place—the anomalous formation of an entire academic discipline around a corpus of literature so small that it can fit comfortably within a single set of book covers.

Theory as Second Honeymoon

Theory in general, moreover, and not just of the cultural kind, has proven handy for coming to terms with the congenital dwarfism of the biblical corpus. Since its debut in biblical studies several decades ago, Theory has regularly been seen as a means of rejuvenating the Bible and the scholars who have taken its name—*biblical* scholars, who thus find themselves wedded to it, for better or worse, richer or poorer, till death, or at least retirement, do them part. In its encounters with biblical studies to date, Theory has largely been seen as a way of defamiliarizing over-familiar material, or getting taciturn texts that tend to use words as if they are on ration, as Auerbach famously argued,[33] to open up. If the Bible is a taciturn conversation partner, a text of few words, Theory helps prevent the conversation from petering out altogether by providing a plethora of new themes on which to chatter (textuality, reader response, gender performativity, colonial mimicry) and a polyphony of new voices to try out (French-accented voices, Indian voices—the opportunities for impersonation are extensive).

Theory also offers other ingenious ways, however, of working with lack, and even of making a virtue of lack—no small part of Theory's appeal for the biblical scholar. For example, the Bible's many blank moments and informational gaps offer ample openings for the reader-

---

33. Erich Auerbach, "Odysseus' Scar," in idem, *Mimesis: The Representation of Reality in Western Literature* (Princeton, N.J.: Princeton University Press, 1953), 3–23.

response critic to fill; its parsimonious and repetitious speech-patterns allow the psychoanalytic critic to fixate on repression and repetition, desire and deferral; while its oblique, often tortuous, modes of argumentation enable the deconstructive critic to obsess about aporetic impasses, logical lacunae, and rhetorical self-sabotage.

Revolutionary Old Discoveries

Theory has found still further uses in biblical studies, as can be seen by once again contrasting its reception there with its reception in literary studies. When Theory arrived in literary studies it entered a discipline that had already produced a rich crop of homegrown meta-reflections on interpretation, as we noted earlier,[34] and was already accustomed to modes of reading and writing that were introspective and performative. The discipline also thrived on independence from method (certainly method in the rigid sense; even the styles of close reading favoured by the New Critics were fluid and supple). When Theory infiltrated biblical studies, however, it arrived in a discipline that was innately historiographical and philological, with no history of reading in the literary-critical sense. Though discussion of the nature of interpretation had, in centuries past, been centered on the fraught space of the biblical text, the division of philosophical-theological and textual labor essential to the invention and development of the discipline of biblical scholarship meant that interpretation theory, such as that of Schleiermacher and Dilthey, was relegated to the separate domain of theological hermeneutics rather than allowed to intrude into the everyday work of the biblical scholar. His allergy to abstraction was the corollary of his obsession with history and fact.

A further attraction of Theory, therefore, for biblical scholars disenchanted with the fact-finding mission of historical criticism was its ability to reintroduce a whiff of abstraction to biblical studies and reopen some fundamental questions of interpretation and epistemology that had long lain undisturbed in the sands of historical-critical positivism. Much that was old took on the sheen of the new. Longstanding problems of philosophy tended to be introduced as revolutionary postmodern discoveries. Old modern relics like Kant were rudely hauled out, charged with believing in unmediated access to the object of inquiry,

---

34. See pp. 15–17 above.

and subjected to public whipping, while Theory received credit for the realization that knowledge of the object can only ever be mediated by the subject. The discovery merited a noisy fanfare in biblical studies and generated considerable argumentative energy, but in ironic unawareness that the structuring of the object of knowledge by the knowing subject had been a very live issue for old man Kant and his periwigged debating partners Leibniz and Hume.

The move was a necessary and strategic one for biblical studies—albeit one that inevitably banalized Theory's contributions to the field. Eagleton tells us that in the professional world that he inhabits as a literary and cultural critic, "assailing absolute truth, objectivity, timeless moral values, scientific enquiry and a belief in historical progress" would be tantamount to flogging a dead horse—or, as he more colorfully puts it, "like firing off irascible letters to the press about the horse-riding huns or marauding Carthaginians who have taken over the Home Counties."[35] In biblical studies, in contrast, the task of "assailing absolute truth," whether of the fundamentalist or historicist variety, and interrogating the premise of the Enlightenment Bible that scientific study would progressively uncover the truth of the biblical object, was entirely apposite and long overdue. Adapting strategically to the demands of this very particular (and rather peculiar) disciplinary context, Theory in biblical studies found itself repeatedly unveiling, with fitting rhetorical flourishes, the discoveries that objectivity is a myth; that interpretation is necessarily an infinite exercise; that exegesis cannot be cleanly separated from eisegesis, nor theology from ideology; and that even our most cautious historical reconstructions are first and foremost imaginative creations. The Theory-redolent name of Hayden White was regularly intoned over the last of these discoveries in particular, but the basic position enunciated in the discovery was commonplace in history departments even in the pre-Theory era, being a fundamental facet of the understanding of historiography expounded by less glamorous names, such as R. G. Collingwood and E. H. Carr.[36]

---

35. Eagleton, *After Theory*, 17.
36. See R. G. Collingwood, *The Idea of History, Revised Edition with Lectures 1926–1928* (ed. Jan van der Dussen; Oxford: Oxford University Press, 1994, first published 1946); E. H. Carr, *What Is History?* (London: Penguin, 1990, first published 1961). Hayden White's most influential work is *Metahistory: The Historical Imagination in Nineteenth Century Europe* (Baltimore: Johns Hopkins University Press, 1973).

Reader-Response Criticism Is No Picnic

In the event, biblical literary critics, the principal translators of Theory into biblical scholarship, did not succeed in straying very far from historical criticism. Reader-response criticism, for instance, made a bigger splash in biblical studies than almost any other development in literary theory,[37] precisely because it could be assimilated surprisingly easily to the historicist ethos of the discipline. Since its arrival in biblical studies,[38] reader-oriented theory has tended to assimilate automatically with the discipline's inbred obsession with the historical author and the historical reader, who, even when ceremoniously renamed the Implied Author and the Implied Reader, are still implicitly shackled to their hypothetical historical contexts, causing reader-response criticism in biblical studies to become an exercise in historical criticism performed

---

37. Exceeded only by narratology, perhaps. Biblical studies books advertising their allegiance to reader-response criticism in their titles (which, however, represent only a fraction of the work influenced by the approach) have included: Robert Detweiler, ed., *Reader Response Approaches to Biblical and Secular Texts* (Semeia, 31; Atlanta: Scholars, 1985); John Paul Heil, *Paul's Letter to the Romans: A Reader-Response Commentary* (Mahwah, N.J.: Paulist, 1987); idem, *The Gospel of Mark as a Model for Action: A Reader-Response Commentary* (2nd ed.; Eugene, Ore.: Wipf and Stock, 2001); Jeffrey Lloyd Staley, *The Print's First Kiss: A Rhetorical Investigation of the Implied Reader in the Fourth Gospel* (SBL Dissertation Series, 82; Atlanta: Scholars, 1988); Philip B. Harner, *Relation Analysis of the Fourth Gospel: A Study in Reader-Response Criticism* (Lewiston, N.Y.: Mellen, 1993); W. Randolph Tate, *Reading Mark from the Outside: Eco and Iser Leave Their Marks* (Bethesda, Md.: Christian University Press, 1995); Randall C. Webber, *Reader Response Analysis of the Epistle of James* (San Francisco: International Scholars, 1996); Bas M. F. Van Iersel, *Mark: A Reader-Response Commentary* (JSNT Supplement Series, 164; Sheffield: Sheffield Academic, 1998); Robert M. Fowler, *Let the Reader Understand: Reader-Response Criticism and the Gospel of Mark* (2nd ed.; Valley Forge, Pa.: Trinity Press International, 2001); Mark Allan Powell, *Chasing the Eastern Star: Adventures in Biblical Reader-Response Criticism* (Louisville, Ky.: Westminster John Knox, 2001); Peter M. Phillips, *The Prologue of the Fourth Gospel: A Sequential Reading* (Library of New Testament Studies; New York: T. & T. Clark International, 2006); Patrick E. Spencer, *Rhetorical Texture and Narrative Trajectories of the Lukan Galilean Ministry Speeches: Hermeneutical Appropriation by Authorial Readers of Luke-Acts* (Library of New Testament Studies; New York: T. & T. Clark International, 2007); and David Paul Parris, *Reception Theory and Biblical Hermeneutics* (Princeton Theological Monograph Series, 107; Princeton, N.J.: Princeton University Press, 2009). For a rare example of a book-length study in reader-response from the field of Hebrew Bible, see A. L. H. M. Van Wieringen, *The Implied Reader in Isaiah 6–12* (Biblical Interpretation Series, 34; Leiden: Brill, 1998).

38. It first arrived with Robert C. Tannehill's "The Disciples in Mark: The Function of a Narrative Role," *Journal of Religion* 57 (1977): 386–405, and yielded its first full-length study in Robert M. Fowler's *Loaves and Fishes: The Function of the Feeding Stories in the Gospel of Mark* (SBL Dissertation Series, 54; Chico, Calif.: Scholars, 1981).

in a wig and dark sunglasses. If poststructuralism has been the preferred form of postmodernism in literary studies, reader-response criticism has been the preferred form of postmodernism in biblical studies,[39] because it enables us to replay old historical and hermeneutical debates in a new register—but not *so* new that the historical questions cease to be important, the big danger with poststructuralism, as most historical critics saw it.

In effect, reader-oriented theory in biblical studies reopened an early-modern can of worms, returning to a fundamental question of readerly freedom that had been raised almost three centuries earlier in relation to the Bible, and then left suspended. Back in the early eighteenth century, thinkers such as Shaftesbury were claiming that the reader should be allowed "the upper hand and place of honour" and that all "readers must be allowed the liberty to read."[40] This campaign for free-reading was bound up with the case for freethinking, and marked the thinker/reader as heterodox. It was also tied to the move to distill divinity from (parts of) the biblical text by singling out the all-too-human author, who, as such, was on the same plane as the reader, and before whom the reader, therefore, did not need to prostrate himself or herself. The freedom of the reader, for Shaftesbury, was postulated on the assumption that the New Testament did not issue from the "immediate pen of that holy founder" Jesus, but from hands that were, as he delicately put it, "differently inspired."[41]

The controversial question of the freedom of the reader was dropped in the project of rehabilitation that was the Enlightenment Bible, or rather taken up only in an anodyne form. Identifying which (human) hands had produced the different strands of text became the focus of scholarly industry, but the relationship of this question to that of the text's author-ity over the reader was left largely unexamined. Indeed, the emergent science of biblical criticism was designed precisely to ward off a plurality of meaning, and hence a plurality of readers, by identifying the true meaning, and making specialist scholars its official guardians. For

---

39. The title of Edgar V. McKnight's 1988 book was symptomatic—*Postmodern Use of the Bible: The Emergence of Reader-Oriented Criticism* (Nashville: Abingdon).

40. Anthony, Earl of Shaftesbury, *Characteristics of Men, Manners, Opinions, Times* (ed. John M. Robertson; introduction by Stanley Grean; New York: Bobbs-Merrill, 1964 [1711, originally 2 vols.]), Book 1, 307.

41. Ibid., 308.

biblical criticism was established in the wake of the perceived disaster of letting the populace at large commune directly with the Bible through such vague and unregulated intermediaries as individual conscience or the Holy Ghost. Vicious inter-Christian conflict and civil war had been the most notable products of free-wheeling free-reading and a general state of affairs in which, as Thomas Hobbes lamented, "every man, nay every boy and wench, that could read English, thought they spoke with God Almighty, and understood what he said."[42] Shaftesbury and other members of the intellectual elite felt that the only viable response to religious violence was to create a sanctioned social space for tolerance and free-reading—but this had to be squared with the unnerving specter of the uncouth hydra-reader beyond the charmed circle of gentleman scholars. Critical biblical scholarship was, to a large extent, invented as a measure for managing these two potentially conflicting readerships. Professionalized philological method emerged as the touchstone and guarantor of valid biblical meaning. Biblical scholarship became a discipline that was narrowly specific in terms of the meaning that could legitimately be attributed to the biblical text, but diffuse in terms of the methods that could legitimately be utilized to mine and refine that meaning.

The particular forms taken by reader-oriented theory in biblical scholarship reflect, in heightened mode, the singularity of meaning and pluralism of approach that has characterized and sustained the discipline for centuries. On the one hand, reader-oriented theory has been harnessed to legitimize the subjectivism of the "approach approach": "You read as a radical feminist, and I'll read as a conservative evangelical; let many flowers bloom." But at the same time it has functioned as the means by which the garden has been fenced and and the flowers pruned. The formalist version of reader-oriented theory that caught on in New Testament studies, in particular, implicitly yokes itself to the quest for authorial intentions (the core enterprise of historical-critical New Testament scholarship since at least the middle of the twentieth century)[43] to the extent that its characteristic preoccupation has been with tracking the progress of the "implied reader" through the text—a

---

42. Thomas Hobbes, *Behemoth, or the Long Parliament* (ed. Ferdinand Tönnies; London: Frank Cass, 1969 [1682]), 21.

43. In Gospel studies, the pursuit of the evangelists' original intentions began to assume central importance with the emergence of redaction criticism. Ironically, 1954

reader who is on a tight leash held by the author, and who jumps obediently through all the readerly hoops that the author has ingeniously
manufactured, with an alacrity and agility that the lumbering herd of
"flesh and blood" readers could never hope to match. Mark Allan Powell, to cite a representative example, constructs the following profile of
the implied audience of Matthew's Gospel:

- Matthew's implied readers are assumed to read the Gospel in
  a normative way—that is, (at least) to read the entire Gospel
  straight through from beginning to end.
- Matthew's implied readers are assumed to know everything that
  the Gospel expects them to know, and they are assumed *not* to
  know anything that the Gospel does not expect them to know.
- Matthew's implied readers are assumed to believe everything
  that the Gospel expects them to believe, and they are assumed
  not to believe anything that the Gospel does not expect them to
  believe.[44]

All of this is very close, as it happens, to the understanding of
interpretation long ago set forth by Schleiermacher, the patron saint
of historical-critical biblical hermeneutics. The reader-response critic's
reader, trotting obediently around the text under the strict control of
the author, essentially embodies Schleiermacher's notion of "congenial-
ity," a state in which the reader recreates the original experience of the
author through that convoluted process termed "the hermeneutic circle." For Scheiermacher, every act of understanding is but the obverse of

---

was the year when the first and most influential work of redaction criticism, Conzel-
mann's elaborate reconstruction of Luke's authorial intentions in reaction to a form-
critical tradition that did not regard the evangelists as bona fide authors, and Wimsatt
and Beardsley's New Critical manifesto declaring a moratorium on the quest for authorial
intentions, simultaneously made their appearance. See Hans Conzelman, *Die Mitte der
Zeit: Studien zur Theologie des Lukas* (Tübingen: Mohr-Siebeck, 1954), and William K.
Wimsatt Jr. and Monroe C. Beardsley, "The Intentional Fallacy," in William K. Wimsatt
Jr., *The Verbal Icon: Studies in the Meaning of Poetry* (Lexington: University of Kentucky
Press, 1954), 2–18.

   44. Powell, *Chasing the Eastern Star*, 75, his emphasis. Powell is, of course, perfectly
well aware that "as real readers, we remain free to approve or disapprove of whatever
effects we decide the narrative is expected to have on us" (ibid.). But this consideration
does not influence his book's exegetical practice.

an act of expression.[45] He argues that such understanding of the biblical texts can be achieved only through intimate familiarity with the historical contexts in which they were written.[46] Implicitly when not explicitly, reader-oriented theory in biblical studies tends to stand in continuity with good solid German hermeneutics, the kind that can always be counted on in a pinch to counter French flightiness or American excess.

Indeed, the brand of reader-oriented theory that has proved most palatable to biblical scholars, and most of all to New Testament scholars, is the German brand, specifically the *Rezeptionsästhetik* of Wolfgang Iser. According to Iser's oft-cited analogy, adapted from Northrop Frye, the literary text "is like a picnic to which the author brings the words and the reader the meaning."[47] This resolves the problem of readerly subjectivity along the same lines essayed by Laurence Sterne—a near contemporary of Shaftesbury, and a favorite of Iser[48]—in his parodic account of reading in *Tristram Shandy* (1757). In Sterne's mock-conciliatory terms, which Iser cites with rather too straight a face, the author should "halve the matter amicably" with the reader and pay compliments to his ingenuity by "leav[ing] him something to imagine in his turn."[49] When Iser himself turns from theorizing, however, to attend to the imaginative task of reading, it quickly becomes clear that the literary picnic is

---

45. Friedrich Schleiermacher, *Hermeneutics and Criticism: And Other Writings* (trans. and ed. Andrew Bowie; Cambridge Texts in the History of Philosophy; Cambridge: Cambridge University Press, 1998), 225–68 passim.

46. Ibid., 231.

47. Wolfgang Iser, *The Act of Reading: A Theory of Aesthetic Response* (Baltimore: Johns Hopkins University Press, 1978), 159.

48. See Wolfgang Iser, "The Reading Process: A Phenomenological Approach," in *Reader-Response Criticism: From Formalism to Post-Structuralism*, ed. Jane P. Tompkins (Baltimore: Johns Hopkins University Press, 1980), 51, and idem, *Laurence Sterne: Tristram Shandy* (trans. David Henry Wilson; Landmarks of World Literature; Cambridge: Cambridge University Press, 1988).

49. Laurence Sterne, *The Life and Opinions of Tristram Shandy* (Harmondsworth: Penguin, 1987), 79. Iser's attempt to assimilate *Tristram Shandy* to his interactive theory of reading ultimately fails to convince. He writes: "Sterne's conception of a literary text is that it is something like an arena in which reader and author participate in a game of the imagination. If the reader were given the whole story, and there were nothing left for him to do, then his imagination would never enter the field. The result would be the boredom which inevitably arises when everything is laid out cut and dried before us. A literary text must therefore be conceived in such a way that it will engage the reader's imagination in the task of working things out for himself, for reading is only a pleasure when it is active and creative. In this process of creativity, the text may either not go far enough, or may go too far, so we may say that boredom and overstrain form the boundaries

not quite the even division of labor that his parable conjures up: the author's picnic hamper is already so abundantly full of rich delicacies, it seems, that all that remains for the reader is to remember to bring a corkscrew.[50]

For biblical scholars, the Bible is just such a picnic basket, overflowing with meanings that the biblical authors have thoughtfully crammed into them and rendering the meanings created by individual readerly subjectivity both unnecessary and unwelcome. Iser's author-oriented critical practice has thus been an excellent fit with traditional biblical-scholarly practice, making his the most attractive version of reader-response criticism on the market.

The potluck character, however, of Iser's reader-oriented reception theory—let the author bring the words and the reader the meaning—while standing in contradiction to his critical practice has been attractive to biblical scholars on other grounds. Such reception theory fits extremely well with the modern notion of the "Liberal Bible." In early modernity, the Bible began to shift, politically, from a forum for autocracy and theocracy into something more recognizably proto-democratic.[51] Modernity does not represent the loss of biblical authority so much as its strategic transformation. One of the major tasks of modern biblical scholarship has been to translate the Bible's erstwhile theocratic authority into a kind of authority more congenial to modernity—moral rather than absolutist authority, based not on arbitrary divine or kingly command but on the self-evident good, to which the modern subject *freely* assents. Reader-response criticism assists in the process of making the Bible more democratic by postulating a power-sharing arrangement between text and reader. The ideology of reader-response criticism is one in which the Bible's meaning is theoretically open to negotiation and mass participation, and it stands in continuity with the ideal of a liberal, democratic Bible. In all democracies, however, freedom is circumscribed no less than it is celebrated. One may

---

beyond which the reader will leave the field of play" ("The Reading Process," 51). Iser's grave appraisal of *Tristram Shandy* seems to miss the fact that its flattery of the reader is strictly tongue-in-cheek. This garrulous novel leaves its reader with as little work to do as the average eighteenth-century gentleman and makes a joke of "boring" him.

50. As we noted earlier; see p. 43.

51. For the early modern invention of the "Liberal Bible," see Yvonne Sherwood, "The God of Abraham and Exceptional States, or the Early Modern Rise of the Whig/Liberal Bible," *Journal of the American Academy of Religion* 76.2 (2008): 312–43.

vote for any candidate in an American presidential election, but only a Republican or a Democrat may win. This political parable better captures the constrained realities of biblical interpretation, and even of biblical reader-response criticism, than the parable of the picnic.

Reader-oriented theory, in the forms favored by biblical scholars, also happens to cohere with certain hallowed themes of Christian theology, notably the delicate balance between free will and predestination within the divine economy. The implied reader's defining address to her author-creator coincides with that of the psalmist to his God: "And in your book were written all the days that were ordained for me, when as yet there was not one of them" (Ps. 139:16, NASB). Within this Augustinian-Calvinist model of reader-response, the Good God and the Good Book graciously grant us freedom—within an ironclad system of constraints. Any bid for any other form of freedom is proscribed in advance as excess and transgression, an abuse of readerly free will and a lapse into Pelagianism: hubristic over-confidence in one's ability to assume full control of one's readerly actions. It would be as though the author were expectantly holding out the hoops that he has carefully crafted but the reader frisks and gambols about, barely noticing them, much less jumping through them. Even the author's sumptuous picnic basket would be ignored, the reader happily munching instead on the sandwiches she has brought with her.

Civil Servants of the Biblical Text

Yet this sad spectacle of the reader's neglect of the author's intent is less common in biblical studies than one might expect, in part because the picnic is always being postponed. A further curious feature of the reception of Theory in biblical studies has been a tendency to defer indefinitely intimate engagement between the Bible and Theory by engaging instead in extensive, earnest, metacritical surveys of the pros and cons of, say, "deconstructionism." Long, chaste courtships seem to be yet another aspect of our ecclesiastical legacy as biblical scholars. It has been our self-revealing habit, as it has not been the habit of secular literary critics, to survey Theories and methodologies from the perspective of *acceptability*: how far is this an acceptable or appropriate Theory or method? Instead of declaring themselves against Theory because it curbs readerly freedom and idiosyncrasy, as Theory's discontents in literary studies are prone to do, surveyors of Theory in biblical studies tend to appeal implicitly to models of sin and consider it a self-evidently damning charge if the practitioners of a certain Theory can be said to be "going too far." A good kind of engagement with Theory—a level-headed survey that would combine a proper appreciation for utility with a salutary caution against going too far (not least on the first date)—is contrasted with a bad kind of engagement with Theory, too much in the thrall of, say, cultish gurus like Derrida or Bhabha. There is something of an institutional anxiety about writing on biblical texts in a strong and audacious way that might identify one as an afficionado and practitioner of raw, unprocessed theory. Theory in mediated and very dilute form—in the form of New Testament narrative criticism, say—becomes the icon of Good Theory, stopping well short of what is assumed (often without reading) to be Theory's wilder, more extravagant side.

Best of all, in some circles at least, is avoiding incriminating associa-tion altogether with the faddish gurus of Theory—and much headache-inducing reading in a field not one's own—by acquiring one's Theory second-hand, with the brand names removed. Thrift-store Theory, if you will. A recent *SBL Forum* article designed to encourage junior schol-ars to eschew narrow specializations and embrace a generalist, inter-disciplinary ethos approvingly echoes Martin Hengel's suggestion that New Testament scholars "attempt to develop an expertise outside of the New Testament."[52] By reading in anthropology or sociology? Or even by reading in Theory? Not quite. "For instance, developing a side interest in certain writings from the Septuagint, Apocrypha, Pseudepigrapha, or Apostolic Fathers would hone one's scholarly skills."[53] But the junior scholar's exposure to the world of ideas beyond the New Testament, and technical scholarship on the New Testament, need not end there. "Read book reviews and summaries of research over a breadth of areas," Bird and Keener urge. "Journals like *Review of Biblical Literature* and *Cur-rents in Biblical Research* can expand one's horizons about the state of scholarship in other fields."[54] And also save one, it is implied, from hav-ing to knuckle down and read such scholarship first-hand.

---

52. Michael F. Bird with Craig Keener, "Jack of All Trades and Master of None: The Case for 'Generalist' Scholars in Biblical Scholarship," *SBL Forum* (May 2009): http://www.sbl-site.org/publications/article.aspx?articleId=820 (accessed August 13, 2009). Cf. Martin Hengel, "Aufgaben der neutestamentlichen Wissenschaft," *New Testament Stu-dies* 40 (1994): 321.
53. Bird and Keener, "Jack of All Trades and Master of None."
54. Ibid.

As a more specific example of thrift-store Theory, consider a recent article in the *Journal of Biblical Literature*, Philippe Guillaume's "Dismantling the Deconstruction of Job."[55] The Theory enthusiast, dully trawling the table of contents of this particular issue of *JBL*, with little expectation of electrification ("Let's see, 'Who Led the Scapegoat in Leviticus 16:21?' . . . "), would likely come awake on encountering Guillaume's title—a knowing allusion, he or she might imagine, to Derrida's equation of deconstruction with dismantling.[56] If he or she were long enough in the tooth, or had read obsessively enough in the annals of early American deconstruction, he or she might even be put immediately in mind of the thrust-and-parry of those heady early days of High Theory—sallies such as J. Hillis Miller's "Deconstructing the Deconstructors," much admired in its time.[57] Our imagined reader might even shake his or her greying head in bemusement at the thought that these second-order deconstructive shenanigans had taken thirty-odd years to migrate into the staid pages of *JBL*.

What bitter disappointment would await our reader, then, once his or her fumbling fingers had found the article. For not only does Guillaume's study not reference any extra-biblical deconstructor, living or dead, it does not even reference any biblical-scholarly attempts to harness extra-biblical deconstruction for the interpretation of Job, such as David Clines's moderately well-known essay "Deconstructing the Book of Job."[58] Instead, Guillaume's article is a response to André LaCocque's "The Deconstruction of Job's Fundamentalism," an earlier *JBL* article that itself does not reference any extra-biblical deconstruction—although it does reference Clines's essay (albeit in passing), so that it is left to Guillaume to effect the absolute watering down of LaCocque's

---

55. Philippe Guillaume, "Dismantling the Deconstruction of Job," *Journal of Biblical Literature* 127:3 (2008): 491–99.

56. As, for example, in his "Letter to a Japanese Friend," trans. David Wood and Andrew Benjamin, in *Derrida and Différance*, ed. David Wood and Robert Bernasconi (Evanston, Ill.: Northwestern University Press, 1988), 3.

57. J. Hillis Miller, "Deconstructing the Deconstructors," *Diacritics* 5:2 (1975): 24–31. Joseph Riddel, the deconstructor who was the particular target of Miller's thrusts, came back with a riposte, "A Miller's Tale," *Diacritics* 5:3 (1975): 56–65, which vertiginously attempted to deconstruct Miller's deconstruction of Riddel's deconstruction of the poetry of William Carlos Williams.

58. David J. A. Clines, "Deconstructing the Book of Job," in *The Bible as Rhetoric: Studies in Biblical Persuasion and Credibility*, ed. Martin Warner (Warwick Studies in Philosophy and Literature; London and New York: Routledge, 1990), 65–80.

already watery brew.[59] All of which serves, at least, to explain the conditions under which article titles with the word "deconstruction" in them can appear in the table of contents of mainstream biblical studies journals such as *JBL*. Such titles can appear only if the word has ceased to mean anything substantive, and is so cut off from anything outside the internal world of biblical scholarly debate that it is all but lifeless from lack of oxygen. In short, they can appear only if the word has become yet another name for biblical historical criticism.

The wholesale poststructuralization of literary studies surely does much to explain its limited impact on biblical studies in recent decades. The varieties of literary criticism that have been most widely embraced in New Testament studies, for instance, are those that assimilate most smoothly with traditional historical criticism, most especially redaction criticism. Narrative criticism, for all its undeniable novelty in the 1980s, seems now in retrospect to have been a singularly painless extension of redaction criticism.[60] What yokes narrative criticism to redaction criticism is a shared preoccupation (ordinarily unstated in the case of narrative criticism) with uncovering the Evangelist's original intentions. The intricate narrative designs that the narrative critic is typically intent on unearthing are precisely those that the Evangelist putatively implanted in the first place. Reader-response criticism, too, at least in the formalist version of it that caught on in New Testament studies (only one of several possible versions, however, as we saw earlier),[61] implicitly harnesses itself to the quest for authorial intentions to the extent that its characteristic preoccupation is with tracking the "implied reader" through the narrative, a reader who is on a tight leash held by the author, as we also saw. Deconstruction, in contrast, in common with other varieties of poststructuralist criticism, characteristically reads against the grain of authorial intentionality, and hence by extension against the definitive recovery project of redaction criticism.

---

59. André LaCocque, "The Deconstruction of Job's Fundamentalism," *Journal of Biblical Literature* 126:1 (2007): 83–97. For the references to Clines, see 92 n. 33; 93 n. 34.

60. For a multifaceted retrospective on Johannine narrative criticism, see Tom Thatcher and Stephen D. Moore, eds., *Anatomies of Narrative Criticism: The Past, Present, and Futures of the Fourth Gospel as Literature* (Resources for Biblical Study, 55; Atlanta: Society of Biblical Literature, 2008). For a detailed critique of Markan narrative criticism, see Scott Elliott, *Reconfiguring Mark's Jesus: Narrative Criticism after Poststructuralism* (Sheffield: Sheffield Phoenix, forthcoming).

61. See p. 43 above.

Deconstruction sticks in the craw of redaction criticism and resists easy incorporation into its maw.

The largely cautious and chaste reception of Theory in biblical studies also seems to betray a fear of writing that stands in stark contrast to secular literary criticism. Literary critics can regularly be found engaging the performative and risky power of words, almost as if they are wilfully confusing the job description of the critic with that of the writer. Critics of James Joyce slip quite comfortably into pun to craft a critical discourse on Joycean writing that itself slides from "syntax" to "sintalks" and shuttles between the "trivial" and the "quadrivial"; while T. S. Eliot scholars have recourse to critical poetry in order to write meaningfully about phrases such as "the intolerable shirt of flame."[62] Nor is this simply an effect of contagion generated by modernist literature. Hoary staples of the literature curriculum, like *Hamlet*, often find themselves written about in works with headings such as "Erasures, Poison, and Nothing," "At the Centre: Wordplay," or "Silence, Soliloquy, Court Speech, Noise"[63]—the kind of thing that happens to Jeremiah, Jonah, or John only rarely and in studies that seem much farther from the center of the discipline than they would be in literary studies. As noted earlier, even self-declared anti-Theorists such as Valentine Cunningham are capable of writing with a stylistic élan that makes most biblical-scholarly prose seem colorless by comparison;[64] while reading "Theoretical" essays such as Kristeva's "Stabat Mater," Cixous's "Bathsheba or the Interior Bible," or certain of Derrida's numerous forays into the Bible plunges us altogether into a mode of critical writing that seems entirely alien to biblical scholarship.[65] What seems so foreign (French as

---

62. As exemplified, say, by the following books, plucked almost at random from the library shelves: Laurent Milesi, ed., *James Joyce and the Difference of Language* (Cambridge: Cambridge University Press, 2003), and John Paul Riquelme, *Harmony of Dissonances: T. S. Eliot, Romanticism, and Imagination* (Baltimore: Johns Hopkins University Press, 1991).

63. All three taken from James L. Calderwood, *To Be and Not to Be: Negation and Metadrama in Hamlet* (New York: Columbia University Press, 1983).

64. See pp. 19–20 above.

65. See Julia Kristeva, "Stabat Mater," in idem, *Tales of Love* (trans. Leon. S. Roudiez; New York: Columbia University Press, 1989), 234–64; Hélène Cixous, "Bathsheba or the Interior Bible," in idem, *Stigmata: Escaping Texts* (London and New York: Routledge, 1998), 3–19. For Derrida's distinctive mode of Bible study, see, for example, Yvonne Sherwood, "Introduction: Derrida's Bible," in *Derrida's Bible* (*Reading a Page of Scripture with a Little Help from Derrida*), ed. Yvonne Sherwood (New York: Palgrave, 2004), 1–20; and

opposed to Anglo-German?) is the slippage into a poetic-philosophical language that "make[s] writing and hearing . . . pair up and dance."[66]

That we don't go in for this kind of thing (much) in biblical studies is clearly not attributable to the kinds of texts we have in front of us. The biblical God and his many amanuenses manipulate words as cavalierly and startlingly as a Joyce or Derrida. Our set texts include the wild writing of the Prophets, texts that muddy the line between oral performance and literary act and so are particularly prone to exploit false etymologies, puns, and the physical shape of words.[67] Then there is the gaudy proto-surrealism of Daniel and Revelation. Even the language of the Gospels is not the colorless, abstract, propositional language of a modern theological treatise; instead the language is consistently concrete, graphic, and pictographic. Standard biblical-scholarly style, meanwhile, functions as a kind of paint-stripper to relieve these pictorial texts of their residual hieroglyphic brilliance.[68]

Our writerly reticence and reserve stems not from the texts on which we write but rather from a fear of breaking with the unwritten regulations that determine our professional style as biblical scholars. For our credibility and authority we rely, more than we might care to admit, on style. Critics such as Steven Shapin and Barbara Shapiro have argued compellingly that truth is in part a social category, and that establishing one's credentials to represent truth, and hence one's credibility, requires conforming to certain distinct social markers, not least stylistic markers and other markers of self-expression.[69] That our herd behavior as biblical scholars includes seasonal clustering in various *societies*—The Society of Biblical Literature, The Society for Old Testament Study, The Studiorum Novi Testamenti Societas—is not accidental. An academic discipline is a collegial body, a social unit, and "fact" is a social as much as an empirical category, established by means of appropriate "episte-

Jay Twomey, "Reading Derrida's New Testament: A Critical Appraisal," *Biblical Interpretation* 13 (2005): 374–403.

66. Hélène Cixous, *Portrait of Jacques Derrida as a Young Jewish Saint* (New York: Columbia University Press, 2004), vii.

67. See Yvonne Sherwood, "Of Fruit and Corpses and Wordplay Visions: Picturing Amos 8.1-3," *Journal for the Study of the Old Testament* 92 (2001): 5–27.

68. See Stephen D. Moore, *Mark and Luke in Poststructuralist Perspectives: Jesus Begins to Write* (New Haven, Conn.: Yale University Press, 1992), 73–85.

69. See Steven Shapin, *A Social History of Truth: Civility and Science in Seventeenth-Century England* (Chicago: University of Chicago Press, 1994), and Barbara Shapiro, "The Concept 'Fact': Legal Origins and Cultural Diffusion," *Albion* 26 (1994): 227–52.

mological decorum."[70] This is the case even, or perhaps especially, with the sciences and those branches of the humanities that aspire to scientific ("unmediated") knowledge.

In biblical studies, epistemological decorum is construed rather differently than in literary studies. In biblical studies, the model of the good reader is the commentator. This self-effacing reader does not write but, as his name implies, merely comments. He is a civil servant of the biblical text. He is a patient laborer in the textual field. He is not a quack, a shyster, or even a salesman. He doesn't need to be. The simple fact that you're already reading, or even consulting, his 800-page commentary on Numbers or Hebrews tells him that you're already sold on the Bible, lock, stock, and barrel, whether for reasons of profession, or piety, or professional piety. For his part, he's so deep into the text as to be all but invisible ordinarily. For hundreds of pages at a time, there's little or nothing in his own text to indicate that it was written by a living, breathing human being. Relative to the life-transforming text that he serves, in any case, the circumstances of his own bookish life are inconsequential. He lives vicariously through the text and willingly under its thrall. This we have on the authority of no less eminent a commentator than Walter Brueggemann:

> This text does not require "interpretation" or "application" so that it can be brought near our experience and circumstance. Rather, the text is so powerful and compelling, so passionate and uncompromising in its anguish and hope, that it requires we submit our experience to it and thereby reenter our experience on new terms, namely the terms of the text. The text does not need to be *applied* to our situation. Rather, our situation needs to be *submitted* to the text for a fresh discernment. It is our situation, not the text, that requires a new interpretation. In every generation, this text subverts all our old readings of reality and forces us to a new, dangerous, obedient reading.[71]

---

70. The term "epistemological decorum" is Shapin's (*A Social History of Truth*, 193–242).

71. Walter Brueggemann, *A Commentary on Jeremiah: Exile and Homecoming* (Grand Rapids, Mich.: Eerdmans, 1998), 18, his emphasis.

Ultimately, of course, Brueggemann is channelling the Protestant Reformers here, not least Luther himself who declared: "This queen [Scripture] must rule, and everyone must obey and be subject to her."[72] The biblical commentator, then, is a humble and obedient servant of Her Majesty, the Queen. As the quintessentially diffident and retiring non-authorial author, he is the direct descendent of the Reformation authors, who have a squirmingly uncomfortable love-hate relationship with the presumed arrogance and Pelagianism of overt authorship, and who often present themselves as smashing the idols of suffocatingly opulent writing (Catholic, of course) in order to establish something that is, in Luther's phrase, *"rain und pur."*[73]

It is not, of course, the case that biblical critics are congenitally more humble than literary critics, or less intent on making a name for themselves and a tower with its top in the heavens; it rather that one makes that name through almost opposite social-writerly rules. Decorum and modesty are high indicators of solidity and respectability, and hence of truth, in biblical studies, as is a posture of obedience to the biblical text and to the inherited traditions of critical biblical scholarship—which is why it is always a good badge of disciplinary membership to accuse a fellow biblical scholar of "going too far," thus marking oneself as one who goes only as far as is proper or necessary and never so far as to appear excessive or unseemly. Such moderation and decorum guarantee good team players who are content to churn out works of scholarship that add but minor variations to already "established" interpretations—the sort of work of which the biblical commentary is emblematic—and thereby move the lumbering disciplinary beast along, step by slow step, though a process of incremental tweaking, poking, prodding, and massaging.

This model of reading, along with its results, is likely to strike our (no less stereotypical and admittedly idealized) literary critic as rather dreary; for in literary studies the inherited social-stylistic model is of the strong, if not flamboyant, authorial signature. In literary studies, credibility is not jeopardized by writing that is self-consciously writ-

---

72. Martin Luther, *Luther's Works*; Vol. 26: *Lectures on Galatians, 1-4* (trans. Jaroslav Pelikan; St. Louis: Concordia, 1963), 57.

73. On *"rain und pur"* ("clear and pure") as an anthem of German Protestant aesthetics, see Peter Matheson, *The Imaginative World of the Reformation* (Edinburgh: T. & T. Clark, 2000), 7.

ing, nor is there an imperative to tie every observation down with the tether of substantiation, suspending footnote after ponderous footnote from the page of the article or monograph[74] until the band of "main" text has grown so dangerously thin that it can barely support the weight of erudition appended to it. (Biblical scholars, for the most part, have not taken early precursors like Pierre Bayle up on their moral critique of the Bible,[75] but our manner of writing is modeled nonetheless on the encyclopedic structure of Bayle's *Dictionary*, where a lonely line of main text frequently floats on a sea of footnotes, and the Bible is both constantly cross-referenced and pushed to the margins by the incessant flood of commentary.[76]) And whereas the author of a commentary or monograph on a biblical text can safely assume that the reader is already a committed consumer of this text, embedded as it is in an entirely inflexible canon, the author of a literary critical study operates in an environment in which canonical boundaries are essentially fluid and periodically subject to renegotiation. The literary critic, unable to assume that the reader is already invested in the text, must devise ever new hooks to grab his or her interest, and is inclined to see critical writing more as an exercise in rhetoric: writing as seduction.

II. Theory in the Second Wave: The Turn to Religion

Let us recapitulate, but also further elaborate, certain points we have already made. The first wave of Theory's advent in biblical studies has, in many ways, restored and revitalized rudimentary philosophical-epistemological debates and, under the banner of the postmodern, reinstated certain forgotten dimensions of the modern. Theory has been obliquely assimilated to the project of the Enlightenment Bible even

---

74. Like certain of the pages in the present monograph. Old habits die hard.

75. See pp. 50–52 above.

76. Compare Sheehan on the Berleburger Bible (1726–40), which he describes as "reams of commentary . . . atop which floated a thin layer of biblical text" (*The Enlightenment Bible*, 74). On the structure of Bayle's *Dictionary*, see Alex Barber, "'I resolved to give an account of most of the persons mentioned in the Bible': Pierre Bayle and the Prophet David in English Biblical Culture," in *Scripture and Scholarship in Early Modern England*, ed. Ariel Hessayon and Nicholas Keene (Aldershot, U.K.: Ashgate: 2006), 235.

while seeming to be in full flight from it or in attack mode against it. But Theory has also succeeded in reviving and expanding dimensions of that project that were earlier suppressed. If the original project of the Enlightenment Bible was consolidated under four fundamental headings—philology, history, aesthetics, and morality[77]—biblical scholarship soon abandoned the aesthetic and the ethical. Theory has revived the aesthetic, in the form of literary criticism, and also the moral, in the form of feminist criticism, ideological criticism, and other approaches that directly engage the ethics or ideologies of biblical texts. Neither revival has thus far resulted in a sweeping transformation of the discipline, however, because truth is still mainly associated with the historical—and not just by scholars. We find, for example, that our own students, though possessed of sensibilities that, in other respects, qualify fully as post-historical, tend, on the whole, to be less scandalized by the charge that the divine command to Abraham to sacrifice Isaac is immoral than by the conjecture that Abraham and Isaac never existed. They similarly express less concern at the fact that Jesus deliberately consigns the masses to ignorance and perdition in Mark 4:11-12 than at the proposal that the pronouncement stems not from the historical Jesus but from the Evangelist.

Marginalizing the Margins

The forms of critical biblical scholarship that evolved out of the eighteenth-century models represented the strategic abandonment of the project of moral criticism for criticism in a more euphemistic sense. Notwithstanding certain rare resumptions of the project (most notably *The Woman's Bible*, as we observed earlier), it is almost as though the nineteenth-century expansion and consolidation of biblical criticism in scientific and historicist modes was designed to avoid uncomfortable moral questions by expending huge scholarly effort elsewhere. And once that tendency took hold, its grip proved extraordinarily tenacious. Only consider historical criticism's apparent opposite (or one of them), liberation theology. Liberation theologians and exegetes have, of course, been centrally concerned with ethical questions. Typically, however, they have not interrogated the ethics of the Bible itself, which is

---

77. So Sheehan, *The Enlightenment Bible*, 91.

something that sets them apart from many postcolonial biblical critics.[78] Terry Eagleton's *After Theory* constitutes a still more striking example of the persistence and pervasiveness, even in critical circles, of a view of the Bible as morally pure. With surprising lack of nuance, Eagleton sets up the Bible as a self-evident opposite to the forces of Fundamentalism and hence as a model of radicalism and social revolution. Of Isaiah, for instance, he writes: "The Book of Isaiah is strong stuff in these post-revolutionary days. It is only left in hotel rooms because no one bothers to read it. If those who deposit it there had any idea what it contained, they would be well advised to treat it like pornography and burn it on the spot."[79] But what if portions of Isaiah (chap. 3, for example) were to be construed as *literally* pornographic, "strong stuff" on other grounds entirely? This is a possibility that seems not to have occurred to Eagleton. In contrast, such thoughts hover permanently on the edge of feminist discourse on the Hebrew Prophets, when they are not central to it. The feminist's Bible is a far more complex reality, ethically speaking, than Eagleton's Bible, notwithstanding his being the product of a literary studies discipline that, for more than half a century, has celebrated the complexity of literary objects—again, testimony to the extraordinary tenacity of the Moral Bible, even on the hyper-critical imagination.

Indeed, it was only in the last quarter of the twentieth century that feminist biblical critics, followed by womanist, ideological, and postcolonial critics, began in earnest to reawaken the moral question from its centuries-long slumber. Even though feminists spearheaded this revival, however, most of them today would be a long way from saying, with an overly optimistic Eagleton, that feminism has "transformed the cultural landscape," at least as far as biblical interpretation, even within the academy, is concerned, and "become the very model of morality for our time."[80] Rather, we would contend, the moral and political force of feminist biblical criticism has become hamstrung by the trope of "reading

---

78. See further R. S. Sugirtharajah, *The Bible and the Third World: Precolonial, Colonial and Postcolonial Encounters* (Cambridge: Cambridge University Press, 2001), 203–75, esp. 240–41. An abridged version of this material is found in Sugirtharajah's *Postcolonial Criticism and Biblical Interpretation* (Oxford: Oxford University Press, 2002), 103–23.

79. Eagleton, *After Theory*, 178. For a trenchant critique of Eagleton's return to religion, see Roland Boer, "Terry Eagleton and the Vicissitudes of Christology," *Cultural Logic* 8 (2005): http://clogic.eserver.org/2005/boer.html.

80. Eagleton, *After Theory*, 13.

as" and the dissipating force of a generic theory of reader-response or text reception that has become fused with identity politics. Reading as a woman, as a feminist, as a womanist, as a *mujerista*, or as a lesbian can be contained (in both sense of the term) within collections of readings "from the margins" or from assorted "social locations," as can reading as a native American of either sex reflecting on the genocidal extirpation of the original inhabitants of the "land of Canaan," or reading as a person of African descent responding to the interpretive history of Genesis 9:20-27 (the so-called "curse of Ham"), or any number of other explicitly contextualized readings. Such collections, along with articles and monographs in this mode, can easily be accommodated to the democratic ethos of the discipline ("You read your way and I'll read my way"; "Let many flowers bloom") and accorded a place in it—but precisely on its margins, where they can be both visible from the mainstream of the discipline and extraneous to it, and need have no deep or lasting effect on how mainstream practitioners of biblical scholarship go about their daily business.[81]

This is not to say, however, that all of these mainstream scholars are unflappably unconcerned about the "reading as" phenomenon and other deviations from the historical-critical paradigm. Tat-siong Benny Liew perceptively notes that the debate concerning minority scholars conducted in the biblical studies mainstream regularly mirrors the immigration debate conducted in the U.S. cultural mainstream. Minority scholars are kept at a distance and suspected of being "migrant workers"

---

81. Sugirtharajah's updated introduction to the third edition of *Voices from the Margin*, appearing fifteen years after the first edition, is tellingly titled "Still at the Margins"— an essay that, with extraordinary speed, mushroomed into a book. R. S. Sugirtharajah, "Still at the Margins," in *Voices from the Margin: Interpreting the Bible in the Third World*, ed. R. S. Sugirtharajah (3rd ed.; Maryknoll, N.Y.: Orbis, 2006), 1–10; idem, *Still at the Margins: Biblical Scholarship Fifteen Years after* Voices from the Margin (New York: T. & T. Clark International, 2008). Other important recent contributions to contextual biblical hermeneutics include Tokunboh Adeyemo, ed., *Africa Bible Commentary* (Grand Rapids, Mich.: Zondervan, 2006); Deryn Guest et al. , eds., *The Queer Bible Commentary* (London: SCM, 2006); Brian K. Blount et al., eds., *True to Our Native Land: An African American New Testament Commentary* (Minneapolis: Fortress Press, 2007); Barbara E. Reid, *Taking Up the Cross: New Testament Interpretation through Latina and Feminist Eyes* (Minneapolis: Fortress Press, 2007); Tat-siong Benny Liew, *What Is Asian American Biblical Hermeneutics? Reading the New Testament* (Honolulu: University of Hawaii Press, 2008); and Randall C. Bailey, Tat-siong Benny Liew, and Fernando F. Segovia, eds., *They Were All Together in One Place? Toward Minority Biblical Criticism* (Semeia Studies, 57; Atlanta: Scholars, 2009).

or "illegal immigrants"—"undocumented" and thus "unqualified"—until they have established their status with appropriate "identification papers" that demonstrate their willingness and competence to employ the mainstream historical-critical methods.[82]

Extrapolating from Liew's observations, we note that just as fretful voices have regularly been raised in the U.S. cultural mainstream concerning the perceived fragmentation of an American culture imagined as formerly homogeneous, and the concomitant threat to a common language (English), so too have fretful voices regularly been raised in the biblical studies mainstream concerning the perceived fragmentation of a field imagined as formerly homogeneous, and the concomitant threat to a common disciplinary language (historical-critical methodology). Representative of such voices is that of Markus Bockmuehl, who laments "the extent to which New Testament scholarship's fragmentation has in recent years been further accelerated by its practitioners' increasingly restricted field of reference and linguistic competence," such practitioners "tend[ing] to concern themselves with primary and secondary literature only in their own postage-stamp-sized bailiwick."[83] Bockmuehl begins his diagnostic and prognostic analysis of the discipline by reflecting at length—and, it should be said, with considerable nostalgia—on C. H. Dodd's 1936 inaugural lecture as Norris-Hulse Professor of Divinity at the University of Cambridge, contrasting the "clear and uncluttered" field of New Testament studies then stretching out before Dodd with the current state of the field.[84] Bockmuehl proposes "the little thought experiment" of whisking Professor Dodd out of his 1930s Cambridge cocoon and into a present-day theological library—specifically, of setting him down before a stack of issues of *New Testament Abstracts* stretching back through the past few decades, and imagining what he might make of what he read in them.[85] To begin with, "Professor Dodd would soon discover that his discipline no longer enjoys any agreement either about the methods of study or even about the criteria by which one might agree about appropriate methods and criteria."[86]

---

82. Tat-siong Benny Liew, "When Margins Become Common Ground," in Sugirtharajah, *Still at the Margins*, 44.

83. Markus Bockmuehl, *Seeing the Word: Refocusing New Testament Study* (Studies in Theological Interpretation; Grand Rapids, Mich.: Baker Academic, 2006), 35.

84. Ibid., 27.

85. Ibid., 30–31.

86. Ibid., 31.

Such fretting about the perceived fragmentation of the field is not uncommon. More remarkable is the lament of R. S. Sugirtharajah, who, in his contribution to *Still at the Margins*, can be heard fretting about the fragmentation of the fragments:

> While once there were Asian, African, Latin American and Indian theologies, these generic theologies have now ruptured into a number of smaller if vibrant discourses. . . . As an illustration, one can cite the case of Indian tribal theology. Once it was simply Indian tribal theology. Now, and rightly, it has expanded into Ao, Khasi, Mizo theologies. . . . While identity hermeneutics has allowed people to empathize with social movements which try to rectify the injustices of the past, the obsessive focus on narrow identity issues may result in the neglect of shared values. . . . One needs to be alert to the likely adverse consequences of the splintering of marginal hermeneutics. It is unlikely that such a fragmented status will radically trouble mainstream biblical study.[87]

More precisely, perhaps, while some in the mainstream may mourn the methodological splintering of the field that has turned historical criticism, until relatively recently coextensive with the field as such, into a fragment of the field, the further fragmentation of the non-historical-critical fragments makes historical criticism, already far and away the biggest fragment, still larger by comparison, a veritable Saturn in relation to the many rings of fragmentary critical phenomena now orbiting it.

The "reading as" phenomenon in biblical studies is also subject to certain philosophical tensions, as we noted earlier.[88] The hermeneutic of pre-given social location yields up readings that are transparently and intentionally local, though across a rather wide span of localities —ranging from the more-or-less specifically local ("'He Must Increase, but I Must Decrease': A Chinese Malaysian Interpretation of John 3:22-30") to the not-quite-local because simply national-as-local ("Hierarchical View of Spirituality in Korean Christian Communities and

---

87. Sugirtharajah, "Muddling Along at the Margins," in idem, *Still at the Margins*, 11.
88. See pp. 70–75 above.

Nicodemus' Spirituality in John"), and from the slightly-surreal local ("Hagar in Finland?") to the Google Earth local ("Jacob Encounters Job on the Streets of Manila").[89] Paradoxically, though such readings are typically motivated by a passion for social justice and human rights, their insistent situatedness and principled distrust of "universals"[90] seems to preclude, or at least complicate and not sit quite comfortably with, appeals to such universal notions as "human rights," which, by definition, are the very antithesis of the ethnic, the cultural, and the local.

Gayatri Chakravorty Spivak has probed such tensions more deeply than most. "'Human Rights' is not only about having or claiming a right or a set or rights," she notes; "it is also about righting wrongs, about being a dispenser of these rights."[91] But "the work of righting wrongs is shared above a class line that to some extent and unevenly cuts across race and the North-South divide."[92] So too is the work of writing biblical readings that are self-consciously local also shared above a class line that to some extent and unevenly cuts across race and the North-South divide. It is a line established by a degree of relative educational privilege. "There is a real epistemic discontinuity between the Southern human rights advocates and those whom they protect," Spivak continues.[93] Likewise, there is a real epistemic discontinuity between the Southern writers of local biblical readings and the subaltern communities on behalf of whom they write. The phenomenon of the *Global Bible Commentary*, a landmark collection of contextual biblical readings, perfectly encapsulates the contradiction we are considering—a contradiction emblazoned, indeed, in the title of the work; for the biblical readings that the *Global Bible Commentary* contains do not, of course, purport to be global but

---

89. All actual paper titles from the two sessions of the Contextual Biblical Interpretation Group held at the Society of Biblical Literature 2009 Annual Meeting in New Orleans. The presenters were Meng Hun Goh, Sung Uk Lim, Kari Latvus, and Jione Havea, respectively.

90. A distrust that comes to especially pointed expression in Bailey, Liew, and Segovia, *They Were All Together in One Place?* "[F]or minority criticism any claim to universality and objectivity emerges as itself subject to contextualization, localized and ideological," the editors affirm in their introduction to the collection (27). The largest section of the collection is entitled "Puncturing Objectivity and Universality."

91. Gayatri Chakravorty Spivak, "Righting Wrongs—2002: Accessing Democracy among the Aboriginals," in idem, *Other Asias* (Oxford: Blackwell, 2008), 14.

92. Ibid., 16.

93. Ibid., 18.

local.[94] And yet they *are* also global to the extent that their conditions of possibility include both the international discourse of critical biblical scholarship and the appeal to such universal notions as justice and human rights. Such local-global readings are vitally necessary, however fraught with contradiction. "One cannot write off the righting of wrongs," insists Spivak.[95] Similarly, one cannot write off the writing of the local in recent biblical scholarship—least of all when such writing is intent on the righting of wrongs.

The practice of reading explicitly out of one's sociocultural location is but one manifestation of the larger phenomenon of identity politics that has taken biblical studies by storm in recent decades—"reading as," as we labeled it earlier. In a debate that has barely begun to spill over into biblical studies (the indented quotation from Sugirtharajah above being a partial, rule-proving exception),[96] literary and cultural Theorists have begun probing the limits of the concept of "identity" (racial, ethnic, gender, sexual, etc.) that has been such a hugely important factor in literary studies since the 1980s and hence in Theory itself. Amanda Anderson, for instance, discusses potential alternatives to a voracious "politics of identity" being "imagined to cover all available intellectual and ethico-political space."[97] Partly in reaction to this problem, Theory began to take an unexpected turn that, as we shall see, entailed a return of certain big old-fashioned words like "universalism" and certain big old-fashioned names like "Kant." One of the next important developments around Theory in biblical studies may be some concerted reflection on how we can think with, as well as against, inheritances of "universality," the thinking *with* it amounting to a thinking *of* it as more or other than

---

94. Daniel Patte et al., eds., *Global Bible Commentary* (Nashville: Abingdon, 2004). Patte notes in his introduction to the volume: "The contributors to the *GBC* are literally from all over the world," approximately (but not coincidentally) two-thirds of them being from the Two-Thirds World. "We, the editors of the *GBC*, asked each of these scholars to address through their commentary the question: 'What is the teaching of the given biblical book for believers in your specific social, economic, cultural, and religious context?'" (xxi).

95. Spivak, "Righting Wrongs," 15.

96. More concerted attempts to grapple with problems arising from the self-fragmenting tendencies of contextual biblical hermeneutics include Bailey, Liew, and Segovia, *They Were All Together in One Place?* (see especially 9–17 in the editors' introduction to the collection), and Elisabeth Schüssler Fiorenza, *Democratizing Biblical Studies: Toward an Emancipatory Educational Space* (Louisville, Ky.: Westminster John Knox, 2009), 23, 89–90, 95, 118–19, 149, 175.

97. Anderson, *The Way We Argue Now*, 5.

a bad old modern thing always and inevitably entailing Eurocentrism, cultural triumphalism, civilising missions, and suppression of the other, and constituting a general, all-purpose alibi for Western imperialism, colonialism, and neocolonialism.

The Return of the Big, Flabby, Old-Fashioned Words

In the first encounters between Bible and Theory, Theory tended to be regarded as secular, sexy, demystifying stuff that adventurous or despairing biblical scholars could import in order to sex up a discipline that seemed hopelessly behind the times. The appeal to, and of, Theory reflected a certain cultural-academic cringe about working in the Bible that was in itself symptomatic of the uncomfortable cultural place that the Bible had come to occupy in the order of knowledge termed "the modern." After all, biblical studies was a discipline whose eponymous object, the Bible, epitomized for the secular Western mindset, more than any other single cultural emblem, the irrational, the delusional, the medieval, the morally questionable, and much else of that unsavory ilk. As such, the Bible also symbolized that which was remote, archaic, and—precisely—behind the times: the time before the modern, the other than the modern. Biblical scholarship itself ceaselessly fed and fattened this conception of the Bible by analyzing it primarily as an ancient document, through methods of analysis that worked hard to be credibly modern, but had the effect of making the Bible the product of a world alien and antithetical to the modern world. Incessant critical labor and the objectivity of scientific methodology set biblical scholarship apart from devotional Bible study (or so we thought, anyway, for a very long time)—marking our emphatic distance from the kind of thing that colleagues in other disciplines tended to imagine we were up to, when they did not imagine outright that we were testifying, praying in tongues, and issuing altar calls in the classroom.

In the first wave of its reception in biblical studies, Theory as academic postmodernism served to scratch our itch to belong fully in the university (while also intensifying that itch, as scratching is prone to do). Theory as a cipher for postmodernism became a means not only of pushing biblical studies more firmly into the "present" but also of propelling it into the "future." What got sidelined in this scramble for critical respectability was the question of how and why the Bible had been constructed as behind (and other to) the modern times in the first place.

Theory came to stand for a "literary" that was "anything but history," but without the important question being asked of why the Bible had become so tightly tied up with history in the first place. Theory became a way of restoring narrativity, the readerly, the writerly, the body, ideology, the ethical, the lyrical, the mystical, the para-rational, and the present to a history-obsessed discipline, without raising the question of how and why the scholar's Bible had become a site from which all of these things had to be excluded.

Something new is emerging between Theory and the Bible that enables us to tackle precisely these kinds of questions. These are questions that have relevance well beyond the boundaries of the tightly demarcated disciplinary fiefdom known as biblical studies. Not coincidentally, therefore, those posing the questions are, almost without exception, not professional biblical scholars. While biblical scholars have been engaging Theory to vamp up a fundamentally old-fashioned and thoroughly untrendy profession, Theorists have been engaging the old uncomfortable relic that is the Bible and have begun using old-fashioned words besides.

Even a partial list of the leading French intellectuals who, since the 1960s, have written on or around the Bible—and, at times, written and Theorized through it—reads like a *Who's Who in High Theory*: Roland Barthes, Hélène Cixous, Gilles Deleuze, Jacques Derrida, Luce Irigaray, Julia Kristeva, Jacques Lacan,[98] Emmanuel Levinas, Jean-Luc Nancy, Michel Serres, and so on.[99] Derrida was the most prolific of these occasional and unorthodox biblical commentators. By his death in 2004 he had written on, or with, such biblical scenes and themes as the creation and fall, the naming of the animals, Cain and Abel, the tower of Babel, Abraham's hospitality to the angels, the "sacrifice" of Isaac, the burial of Sarah, the wandering in the desert, "shibboleth," the tactile Synoptics and the touch-phobic Fourth Gospel, Jesus' healings of the blind, the Last Supper, doubting Thomas, the conversion of Saul/Paul, and the Apocalypse of John.

---

98. "Writing" through his amanuensis Jacques-Alain Miller.

99. Many of these writings are either summarised in *The Postmodern Bible* (those of Barthes, Derrida, Lacan, Kristeva, and Irigaray) and/or anthologized in *The Postmodern Bible Reader* (those of Barthes, Cixous, Derrida, Kristeva, Lacan, Levinas, and Serres). See The Bible and Culture Collective, *The Postmodern Bible*, and David Jobling, Tina Pippin, and Ronald Schleifer, eds., *The Postmodern Bible Reader* (Oxford: Blackwell, 2001).

Beginning in earnest in the 1990s, however, Theory, Bible, and religion began to try out some new steps. Derrida led the dance, as much as anybody, and at an age when he might have been content to sit it out. During the last decade or so of his life, Derrida's previously muted interest in religion, including biblical religion, intensified and took several new turns.[100] Meanwhile, other prominent European intellectuals, notably Alain Badiou, Giorgio Agamben, and Slavoj Žižek were busily Theorizing with, of all things, the theology of Saint Paul, following in the footsteps of Jacob Taubes.[101] By 2005, Stanley Fish was announcing in *The Chronicle of Higher Education* that "high theory" and the "triumvirate of race, gender and class" were fast being ousted by "religion" as the "new center of intellectual energy."[102] Ironically, given Derrida's leading role in Theory's turn to religion, Fish relates the (supposed) death

---

100. See especially Jacques Derrida, *The Gift of Death* (trans. David Wills; Chicago: University of Chicago Press, 1995); idem, *Acts of Religion* (ed. Gil Anidjar; London and New York: Routledge, 2002); and Jacques Derrida and Gianni Vattimo, eds., *Religion* (trans. David Webb et al.; Stanford, Calif.: Stanford University Press, 1998). The full list of relevant work would be quite long.

101. See Alain Badiou, *Saint Paul: The Foundation of Universalism* (Cultural Memory in the Present; trans. Ray Brassier; Stanford, Calif.: Stanford University Press, 2003); Giorgio Agamben, *The Time That Remains: A Commentary on the Letter to the Romans* (Meridian: Crossing Aesthetics; trans. Patricia Dailey; Stanford, Calif.: Stanford University Press, 2005); Slavoj Žižek, *The Puppet and the Dwarf: The Perverse Core of Christianity* (Short Circuits; Cambridge, Mass.: MIT Press, 2003); Jacob Taubes, *The Political Theology of Paul* (Cultural Memory in the Present; trans. Dana Hollander; Stanford, Calif.: Stanford University Press, 2004). Taubes's book emerged from a series of lectures delivered in 1987. Another notable "Theoretical" encounter with Paul occurs in Jean-François Lyotard and Eberhard Gruber, *The Hyphen: Between Judaism and Christianity* (Philosophy and Literary Theory; trans. Pascale-Anne Brault and Michael Naas; Amherst, N.Y.: Humanity, 1999), esp. 13–28. Also see Douglas Harinck, ed., *Paul, Philosophy, and the Theopolitical Vision: Critical Engagements with Agamben, Badiou, Žižek and Others* (Eugene, Ore.: Cascade, 2010); John D. Caputo and Linda Martin Alcoff, eds., *St. Paul among the Philosophers* (Indiana Series in the Philosophy of Religion; Bloomington: Indiana University Press, 2009); and John Millbank, Slavoj Žižek, and Creston Davis, with Catherine Pickstock, *Paul's New Moment: Continental Philosophy and the Future of Christian Theory* (Grand Rapids, Mich.: Brazos, 2010). Jean-Luc Nancy, for his part, snubs Paul to philosophize instead with "The Epistle of Saint James" (*Dis-Closure: The Deconstruction of Christianity* [Perspectives in Continental Philosophy; trans. Bettina Bergo et al.; New York: Fordham University Press, 2008]), while Žižek has recently deployed the Book of Revelation to analyze the terminal stages of late capitalism (*Living in the End Times* [London: Verso, 2010]).

102. Stanley Fish, "One University Under God?" *The Chronicle of Higher Education*, January 7, 2005: http://chronicle.com/article/One-University-Under-God-/45077 (accessed March 30, 2010).

of High Theory and the rise of religion to the (literal) death of Derrida. Fish credits himself with having earlier hazarded the unexpected
answer "religion" when asked to comment on what might possibly come
after Theory, that is, after Derrida. Biblical scholars who know Fish, if
they know him at all, as the author of *Is There a Text in This Class?*[103] and
hence as an arch-debunker of all that biblical scholars have tended to
assume about the recoverability of textual meaning, including biblical
meaning, may be surprised to find him now urging academics to "take
religion seriously," that is, "to regard it not as a phenomenon to be ana-
lyzed at arm's length, but as a candidate for truth," and tinkering with
the professional/confessional separation in an opinion piece with the
title "One University Under God?" These are indeed topsy-turvy times
for literary academia.

What Derrida, the Paul-infatuated continental philosophers, and
sundry other participants in this unlikeliest "return to religion" were up
to—all differently, however—can best be understood by contrasting it
with what Theory-besotted biblical scholars were up to during roughly
the same period. Biblical scholars were busy applying Theory understood—as it also tended to be in 1980s literature departments—as an
extension of a very modern practice of demystification or secularization.[104] Meanwhile certain Theorists were busy interrogating the idea of
secularization and all its supporting structures, deliberately begging the
question by insistently returning us to "religion."[105] While Theory was
being plundered in biblical studies for vogueish neologisms and modish

---

103. An important work for biblical literary criticism in the 1980s. See Stanley E.
Fish, *Is There a Text in This Class? The Authority of Interpretive Communities* (Cambridge, Mass.: Harvard University Press, 1980).

104. The present authors would unhesitatingly number themselves among these
biblical scholars. Sherwood would classify her early work as an exercise in demystification or secularization. Fresh from an English Literature department, she regarded the
conjunction of Bible and Theory as something akin to the coupling of a prophet and a
prostitute: religious object meets "secular" Theory in an impious, and rather exciting,
clash. While exposing the deconstructive fragility of violent hierarchies within the Bible,
she left foundational disciplinary and modern hierarchies firmly intact, not least that
between the modern subject and the religious object. Moore, meanwhile, was staging
parallel secularizing demystifications of the biblical God and biblical God-talk, but again
in ways that necessitated a tidy separation between the modern (and even the postmodern) subject and the religious object.

105. For an important recent example of such work, see Talal Asad, Wendy Brown,
Judith Butler, and Saba Mahmood, *Is Critique Secular? Blasphemy, Injury, and Free
Speech* (Berkeley and Los Angeles: University of California Press, 2009). See also the

"post-"isms, Theory outside of biblical studies was turning away from neologisms toward big bad old-fashioned words, among them universalism, democracy, humanism, religion, faith, belief, Christianity, the messianic, Saint Paul, truth, justice, forgiveness, friendship, the kingdom, the neighbor, hospitality, and even, for God's sake, evil.[106] Theory vaults disrespectfully over modern boundaries between the religious and the political, the confessional and the professional, the private and the public, and the believer and the citizen that have been erected for our safety and security. At the same time, by extension, it absolutely fails to observe the proper distance of (historical) critique and treat the Bible in ways that can seem, to the professionally trained biblical scholar,

---

various postings on the topic of the secularity of critique on "The Immanent Frame: Secularism, Religion, and the Public Sphere" (http://blogs.ssrc.org/tif).

106. See, for example, Jacques Derrida, *Deconstruction in a Nutshell: A Conversation with Jacques Derrida* (ed. John D. Caputo; New York: Fordham University Press, 1997)—the conversation circles around such themes as justice and the messianic; idem, *Politics of Friendship* (trans. George Collins; London: Verso, 1997); idem, *Of Hospitality* (trans. Rachel Bowlby; Stanford, Calif.: Stanford University Press, 2000); idem, *On Cosmopolitanism and Forgiveness* (trans. Mark Dooley and Michael Hughes; London and New York: Routledge, 2001); and idem, *Rogues: Two Essays on Reason* (trans. Pascale-Anne Brault and Michael Naas; Stanford, Calif: Stanford University Press, 2005), which is on "the democracy to come." See also the works listed in n. 101 above, and, in addition, *differences* 7:1 (1995), which included Joan W. Scott, "Universalism and the History of Feminism" (1–14), Noami Schor, "French Feminism Is a Universalism" (15–47), and Etienne Balibar, "Ambiguous Universality" (48–74); Ernesto Laclau, "Universalism, Particularism, and the Question of Identity," in *The Identity in Question*, ed. John Rajchman (London and New York: Routledge, 1995), 93–108; Hent de Vries, *Philosophy and the Turn to Religion* (Baltimore: Johns Hopkins University Press, 1999); idem, ed., *Religion: Beyond a Concept* (The Future of the Religious Past; New York: Fordham University Press, 2007); Judith Butler and Slavoj Žižek, eds., *Contingency, Hegemony, Universality: Contemporary Dialogues on the Left* (London: Verso, 2000); Alain Badiou, *Ethics: An Essay on the Understanding of Evil* (trans. Peter Hallward; London: Verso, 2001); Slavoj Žižek, *The Fragile Absolute: Or, Why Is the Christian Legacy Worth Fighting For?* (London: Verso, 2001); idem, *On Belief* (Thinking in Action; London and New York: Routledge, 2001); Slavoj Žižek and John Milbank, *The Monstrosity of Christ: Paradox or Dialectic?* (ed. Creston Davis; Short Circuits; Cambridge: MIT Press, 2009); Jean-Luc Nancy, *Corpus* (trans. Richard A. Rand; Perspective in Continental Philosophy; New York: Fordham University Press, 2008); idem, *Noli me tangere: On the Raising of the Body* (trans. Sarah Clift; New York: Fordham University Press, 2008); Terry Eagleton, *On Evil* (New Haven, Conn.: Yale University Press, 2010); Elizabeth Weed and Ellen Rooney, eds., "Humanism," special issue of *differences* 14:1 (2003); and "The Dark God," special issue of the hyper-Theoretical psychoanalytic journal *UMBR(a)* 1 (2005), whose editorial is entitled "The Object of Religion" and whose back jacket issues the challenge, "I defy all of you: I can prove to you that you believe in God's existence."

disturbingly intimate, proximate, or "philosophical." Such modes of engagement with the Bible conjure up the ghosts of certain others expelled early on from the purified disciplinary space that is modern biblical scholarship.

The "(re)turn to the Bible" entailed in this larger "(re)turn to religion," so called, does not promise or threaten a renaissance or revival of the Bible in any sense that confessional communities would readily recognize, nor does it simply reenact the conviction that we must all engage with the Bible somehow as towering cultural artifact because we cannot get around it or get over it (the foundational premise of the Enlightenment Bible, as well as the source of our monthly paychecks as biblical professionals). Rather, in the wake of Theory (in both senses of the phrase), the Bible is coming to be seen as a key site where foundational, but unsustainable, "modern" separations were made. What might this mean for biblical scholarship per se? By engaging anew with the formative history of our discipline, we can investigate and interrogate the process whereby critical discourse on the Bible became a means for the consolidation of certain antitheses foundational to modernity, such as religion and reason, myth and history, theology and philosophy, the cultural and the universal, modern subject and ancient object.

Jonathan Sheehan's *The Enlightenment Bible* offers one example of such study. It is not yet another self-congratulatory aetiological saga of the evolutionary process whereby *homo biblicus academicus*, taking his first unsteady steps in early modern Europe, began to walk upright, to jog, and then to run, eventually arriving at the present, to be cheered and applauded by all his descendants. Rather, it is an investigation of the broader cultural negotiations that took place in the sixteenth through the nineteenth centuries around the Bible as symptomatic cultural space. A still more incisive example of such study—because more informed, and formed, by Theory—is Ward Blanton's *Displacing Christian Origins*, which argues that we need a "radical engagement" with our own "disciplinary history" if Theory is ever going to generate anything more than a series of "sideshow[s] at the SBL."[107] In a canny demonstration of what the relationship between Bible and Theory might become—or of one form, at any rate, that it might take—Blanton uses nineteenth- and

---

107. Ward Blanton, *Displacing Christian Origins: Philosophy, Secularity, and the New Testament* (Chicago: University of Chicago Press, 2007), 17.

twentieth-century debates about Christian origins to talk about such issues as the "enabling break" between the secular subject and the religious object; philosophy's allergy to positive religion (including the separation of philosophy and the Bible); and how biblical criticism came to obsess about the "danger" of narcissistically projecting oneself into the text, such projection, however, ironically functioning as the very "possibility for the continuation of the guild."[108] In Blanton's book, seminal biblical critics such as Strauss, Schweitzer, and Deissmann engage with seminal modern philosophers such as Hegel, Nietzsche, and Heidegger in a dialogue moderated by Derrida, Žižek, Agamben, and other contemporary Theorists. This strong encounter between Bible and Theory contrasts starkly with the weak use of Theory in certain forms of biblical literary criticism that surreptitiously revert back to the truisms on which biblical scholarship has always thrived, as we argued earlier, such as the contamination of the historical object by the contemporary subject, who is never quite objective enough.

As work such as that of Agamben, Badiou, Derrida, Nancy, and Žižek outside the field of biblical studies, work such as that of Blanton within it, and work such as that of John Caputo on its margins suggests,[109] the Bible, like religion, is now being used a resource for philosophers to think beyond the limits of empiricism, ontology, and metaphysics. The "(re)turn to the Bible" in Theory and philosophy—or philosophical Theory—is, however, a move that constitutes a philosophical scandal, since it seeks to include within modern philosophy that which, by modern philosophy's own self-definition, must necessarily be excluded from it. The Bible has become a resource for unsettling settled identities and shaking up the way we think about established concepts. Badiou, for instance, uses the Pauline corpus to produce alternative ways of conceptualizing such foundational notions as universalism and the subject, and to critique "identitarian fanaticism" which, he

---

108. Ibid., 52–53.

109. See especially John D. Caputo, *The Weakness of God: A Theology of the Event* (Indiana Series in the Philosophy of Religion; Bloomington: Indiana University Press, 2006). Caputo is a philosopher of religion and his principal interlocutors in this book are Derrida, Paul, and Jesus. Yet another fruitful model is provided by the recent work of the literary and cultural critic Regina Schwartz. See especially her "Revelation and Idolatry: Holy Law and Holy Terror," *Genre* 150 (Spring/Summer 2007): 1–16, which employs Badiou and (later) Derrida in a highly sophisticated reading of the Exodus narrative, one in which the narrative challenges the Theory even as the Theory analyzes the narrative.

argues, promotes capitalism's globalizing project.[110] "Saint Paul" thereby becomes (and not just for Badiou, as we have seen) an exceedingly unlikely but extremely productive site where contemporary Theoretical questions—in this case, the limits of identity and the possibility of the universal—are hashed out.

What such studies further suggest is that we are on the cusp of more significant and more searching engagements between Bible and Theory than before—engagements that promise more than further neologisms, "post"-isms, and the Next Big Thing or the Latest (Grotesquely Adjectivized) Big Name ("Toward a Žižekian Reading of Zephaniah"; "Acts in Agambenian Perspective"). These impending encounters have the potential to push the conjunction of Bible and Theory beyond rote readings of the biblical texts in which everything that may be said or thought has already been determined in advance by our disciplinary DNA. One dimension of this renewed encounter with Theory (the most obvious dimension, perhaps) would take its lead from recent reactivations of the Bible in Theory and engage with and extend what philosophers, in particular, have been doing with the Bible, while resisting the temptation simply to repeat the protective mantra that they are not reading Paul, say, as they should (read: as we would). This reflex gesture reinforces the proprietary wall that biblical specialists have always erected around the Bible, ensuring in advance that any engagement with Theory will remain strictly superficial and ultimately inconsequential.

A further dimension of this intensified encounter with Theory would be a revisiting of our own disciplinary origins—not for the purpose of performing yet another recital of the epic emergence and ascent of our scholarly tribe, however, designed to explain and legitimize the styles of biblical scholarship that most of us still practice. This is perhaps the most necessary dimension of our renewed encounter with Theory, since a discipline's myth of origins powerfully predetermines its practice. Our purpose would be to pick the locks of the disciplinary mechanism itself and expose its inner operations; to probe the discomfort zones that mark the edges of acceptable and normative practice in our guild; to examine the system of exclusions that constitute our professional identities as biblical scholars; and to reflect on how precisely this system relates to that order of knowledge we call "modern." Whereas what might be

---

110. Badiou, *Saint Paul*, 5–7.

called the first wave of engagement between Bible and Theory promised new postmodern gadgets to affix to the same old disciplinary machine, what might be called the second wave of engagement between Bible and Theory does not. This second wave would thus have little to contribute to reflections on "the future of biblical studies" or "biblical scholarship in the twenty-first century"—a critical subgenre that has tended overwhelmingly to think in terms of the discipline's continued survival and self-sustenance through continued methodological innovation, and that typically translates into advocacy for those new methods that seem to sit most solidly and securely upon the foundations established by the older methods. Instead, this second wave would enable metacritical analyses of our disciplinary pasts that would radically dismantle the default categories in which we operate as biblical scholars, and thereby enable modes of biblical analysis that cannot at present easily be envisioned.

Admittedly, this is hardly a comfortable prospect. But it is precisely in this self-risking mode that the engagement between Bible and Theory promises intellectual relevance beyond our own self-replicating disciplinary enclave. The turn for which we are calling is also an ironic twist, for we stand to gain this broader academic relevance as biblical scholars by the most unlikely means imaginable. We need to find religion.

Index of Names